ONE LONG LINE OF MARVEL

ALAN HUSTAK

One Long Line of Marvel

200 Years of Montreal's
St. Patrick's Parade

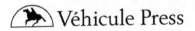 Véhicule Press

Published with the generous assistance of the Canada Council for the Arts and the Canada Book Fund of the Department of Canadian Heritage.

 Canada Council   Conseil des arts
for the Arts   du Canada   Canadä

Cover design by Brian Morgan
Cover photo by Alan Hustak
Set in Minion by Simon Garamond

Dépôt légal, Library and Archives Canada and the Bibliothèque national du Québec, first trimester 2024
The publisher is pleased to acknowledge any unacknowledged property rights.

LIBRARY AND ARCHIVES CANADA CATALOGUING IN PUBLICATION

Title: One long line of marvel : 200 years of Montreal's St. Patrick's Parade / Alan Hustak.
Names: Hustak, Alan, 1944- author.
Identifiers: Canadiana (print) 20230557287 | Canadiana (ebook) 20230557309 | ISBN 9781550656589 (softcover) | ISBN 9781550656626 (EPUB)
Subjects: LCSH: Saint Patrick's Day—Québec (Province)—Montréal—History. | LCSH: Parades—Québec (Province)—Montréal—History.
Classification: LCC GT4995.P3 H87 2024 | ddc 394.26209714/28—dc23

Published by Véhicule Press, Montréal, Québec, Canada
www.vehiculepress.com

Distribution in Canada by LitDistCo
www.litdistco.ca

Distribution in US by Independent Publishers Group

www.ipgbook.com

Printed in Canada

In memory of Margaret Healy, (1931-2020)
and Don Pidgeon (1937-2016)
who adopted me into their extended
Irish family

Kevin Cassidy with his canine friend at the 1966 parade.

Contents

APPENDICES

Foreword

AS PRESIDENT OF THE United Irish Societies of Montreal (Organizers of the Montreal St. Patrick's Parade), it is with great pride and enthusiasm that I welcome you to this unique journey through the history of one of the most cherished traditions in our beloved city.

For well over a century, the Montreal St. Patrick's Parade has been a symbol of unity, a testament to the rich tapestry of the Irish community, and a celebration of Irish heritage in the heart of Quebec. This parade has not only withstood the test of time but has flourished, becoming an annual spectacle that brings together people from all walks of life, across multiple cultures, and fostering a sense of togetherness that defines our city.

As you read through the book, you will travel; through time, and explore the origins of the Montreal St. Patrick's Parade. From humble beginnings, the parade has evolved into a grand procession that captures the imagination and hearts of Montrealers and visitors alike.

Through its pages, you will meet the characters, the volunteers, and the dedicated individuals who have worked tirelessly to keep this tradition alive. The stories shared here are a testament to the passion and commitment of those who have dedicated their time and energy to ensure the parade's continued success.

But this book is more than just a historical account; it is a celebration of the Montreal St. Patrick's Parade's enduring spirit. It is a reminder of the joy it brings to the faces of children and adults alike, as they gather along the parade route, clad in green, to cheer on the vibrant floats, marching bands, and cultural performances that make our parade a truly exceptional event.

As the future moves on, with the St. Patrick's Parade in Montreal there is a growing awareness of one's roots now more than ever in the past due to DNA research. Most people do not know that 40% of Quebecers have Irish roots and this will serve the community well for the next generation since people are aware of what a jewel we have right here in Montreal.

I hope this book serves as a tribute to the past, a celebration of the present, and an inspiration for the future of the Montreal St. Patrick's Parade. May it continue to bring joy, laughter, and a sense of belonging to all who are fortunate enough to be a part of this remarkable tradition.

Kevin Tracey
President, United Irish Societies of Montreal

Introduction

FEW PARADES CONSISTENTLY generate as much enthusiasm as Montreal's annual St. Patrick's Parade. As a street carnival it has outlived the *patriote* rebellion of 1837, Fenian infiltration, Orange animosity, strained relationships among Roman Catholic priests who wanted to have it cancelled, two World Wars, two Quebec independence referendums, three years of the COVID-19 pandemic, and two centuries of howling March winds and chilling subzero temperatures. For, as the *Montreal Star* observed in 1871, "Ireland's great day was fixed unfortunately in a month particularly unfavourable for outdoor displays of enthusiasm." Yet organizers seem to take perverse pride in holding the late winter parade to commemorate Ireland's patron saint no matter what the weather or the political winds. It claims not to be political, but politicians of every stripe have made it a point to walk in it to further their ambitions.

It has been said residents spend six months of the year waiting for the parade to happen then spend the next six months talking about how great the last one was. There is something repetitive in all parades but in each unfolding year they are all unique. Like the shape shifters and other supernatural creatures in Irish mythology Montreal's St. Patrick parade has over two centuries remained rooted in the Irish soul and connected to Irish tradition.

Almost everything that we know of the bishop who inspired it is conjecture. Patrick reveals himself to us in his writings as an affectionate, humble, deeply sensitive fifth-century missionary priest of inexhaustible courage. "I Patrig, a sinner, am the most ignorant and of least account among the faithful," he wrote in his Confessions. "I owe it to God's grace that so many people through me should be born again to Him."

Patrick was never officially canonized a saint in the Roman Catholic Church, but, in 1631 Pope Urban VIII officially declared that he was "an apostle of Ireland." By the end of the 17th century the observance of St. Patrick's Day had grown into what one visitor to Ireland, Thomas Dinley, called "an immovable feast when Irish of all stations and conditions wear crosses in their hats, some of green ribbon, and the vulgarly superstitious wear shamrocks which they likewise eat to cause (they say) a better breath."

Montreal's parade began in 1824 as so much paddy-whackery and evolved into a commercialised community blowout that reflects the spirit of the Irish diaspora, which at times has devolved into an embarrassing caricature of what it means to be Irish.

There are, however, accounts of gatherings in Quebec as early as 1819. The day's religious overtones have long disappeared and "Paddy"—never "Patty" please—has now become a secular, pop-cultural icon. The wearing of green is ingrained as a civic festival which each year unites Montreal's diverse population in an exuberant rite of winter's last gasp. It has become the people's parade—Montreal's Mardi Gras, where the bystanders have become as equally important to its success as the participants.

The Irish are great storytellers who sometimes tend to bend the facts a little to embellish their history. Organizers have for years boasted that Montreal's parade has taken place continuously without interruption. Although the 200th anniversary is in 2024, there have only been 195 parades since 1824. For the record, the parade has been officially cancelled five times in its 200-year history: in 1878—ostensibly in mourning for Pope Pius IX, (but there is more to that story in Chapter Six); in 1902 out of respect for Father John Quinlivan, the pastor of St. Patrick's who died in Paris in March of that year; in 1918, to mourn the death of the troubled Irish patriot John Redmond; and in 2020 and 2021 because of COVID-19. It was officially cancelled in 1948 when it was rained out, but an "outlaw" parade went ahead anyway.

What is impressive is how such a relatively small group of dedicated volunteers is responsible for staging so big a celebration each year. About 20 members on the parade committee spend all year working out the logistics of each parade. "We have a regular cast of characters, and we're very careful about who we allow in the parade," says Patty McCann, a parade director for ten years and chief reviewing officer of the 2024 parade. "Planning never really stops. There is always somebody doing something, but the line up isn't nailed down until the end of January." One of the biggest challenges, she says, is lining up the par-ticipants, and making certain animals aren't near brass bands. About 80 marshals are responsible for maintaining order during the parade. The parade committee is supported by the UIS executive and its membership who assume responsibilities for judging the floats, parade security, and other assignments.

Chapter One

IMAGINE IN YOUR MIND'S eye, if you will, some of those uniformed Irish veterans of the War of 1812 who swaggered into dinner at Swords' Hotel in Old Montreal on March 17, 1824, to celebrate St. Patrick's Day. There were about thirty guests present including Major Michael O'Sullivan, who thought it "shameful that St. Patrick's Day had never before been met with a public celebration in Montreal" and who organized the gathering. The major had distinguished himself at the Battle of Châteauguay in which a Canadian force repelled an attempted American invasion of Canada in 1813. Also at the table was Benjamin Holmes, the manager of the Bank of Montreal, undoubtedly wearing his old Canadian Light Dragoons regimental uniform as he raised his glass and drank the more than 20 toasts that were proposed during the evening.

It is safe to assume that Jocelyn Macartney Waller, the dangerously provocative editor of the *Canadian Spectator*, was present, as was James O'Donnell, the New York-based Anglican architect from County Wexford, who arrived in Montreal to begin work on what would be his masterpiece, Notre Dame Church on Place d'Armes.

These were elite, professional men rewarding themselves for their stewardship and their common Irish ancestry. In 1824, about one in five of Montreal's residents were of Gaelic Irish extraction; but conspicuous by their absence from the lavish dinner were the unskilled blue-collar Roman Catholic Irish immigrants who had been working for three years on the construction of the Lachine Canal. The Irish were the largest group of carters and day labourers employed on the project, but tradesmen were not included as part of Montreal's established loyalist, conservative, Anglo-Irish community. One of the earliest published accounts of a St. Patrick's Day gathering was in 1819, when "a select company" sat down to a table groaning under the weight of every seasonable delicacy. "The juice of the grape flowed from the welcome goblet, inspiring all with harmony and delight. At a late hour the company separated with scarce any other feelings than the anticipation of the return of this anniversary; and cold must have been the heart who could have left such a scene without a feeling of affectionate goodwill toward the happy Sons of the sea-girt Emerald Isle."

Archival accounts have been lost in a fire, but we may presume that members of the city's merchant class held such dinners each year until 1824 when the parade was launched. The founding parade dinner was described as "a wine inspiring scene." Those in attendance, according to the *Gazette,* were "brought together on a joyous occasion, united by one liberal feeling, untainted by either religious or national prejudices, all seemed united in brotherly love."

Those present were a fraternity of some of Montreal's most prominent Irishmen, both Catholic and Protestant. There were toasts to the Patron Saint of course, then four toasts to the Royal family—King George IV, Queen Caroline, Princess Charlotte, and the Duke of Clarence (heir to the throne). Other toasts followed: the toast to "the day and all those who honour it," the toast to the "Green Immortal Shamrock," toasts to Saint Andrew, and to St. George. They drank toasts to the health of Lower Canada, Upper Canada, Atlantic Canada, to Orators and Poets, to immigrants, to the Garrison, to the Fair sex, to all guests present, to the clergy. The last toast was "to our next meeting." These men were Irish to the core, but many of them had repelled an American invasion of Canada, and from a local perspective, they were proud of their contributions to the Crown and to the colony.

If it hadn't been for that dinner, Montreal's St. Patrick's Day Parade may well not have happened. After the meal the lubricated crowd made its way from Swords' Hotel along St. Paul Street to "The Regillie," the old Recollect chapel at the corner of Ste. Helene and Notre-Dame Streets.

O'Sullivan, the man who organized the event, was a pugnacious Tipperary Irishman and prominent Montreal lawyer who had come to Quebec as a youngster. He was educated by Sulpicians and articled in law with Major Denis Benjamin Viger, another veteran of the war of 1812. During the war O'Sullivan served as aide-de-camp to Charles Michel d'Irumberry de Salaberry, an officer in the British army. When the war ended, O'Sullivan was elected a member of the legislative council for the district of Huntingdon where originally, he had aligned himself with French-Canadian *patriotes*. He counted Louis-Joseph Papineau among his closest friends.

O'Sullivan walked with a painful pronounced limp, the scars not of battle, however, but scars from a celebrated duel with a military surgeon, William Caldwell that he survived six years earlier. In 1819, O'Sullivan was at odds with Caldwell, a Scot Presbyterian, who was raising money for a Protestant hospital in Montreal. O'Sullivan maintained that money could be better spent on enlarging the Hôtel Dieu, a Roman Catholic institution. O'Sullivan made it clear that he didn't trust English doctors to do a better job than the French who had operated the Hôtel Dieu for 174 years. In a letter to the editor, Caldwell accused O'Sullivan of cowardice. The two men engaged in a duel with pistols at Windmill Point on April 11, 1819. Both men survived, but because of the notoriety, by 1824, Sullivan was among the most prominent Irishmen in the city.

By 1828, it appears St. Patrick's Day celebrations had become an annual event, and that year as advertisements to celebrate "the festival of the 'Tatelar niall of Ireland'" (punctual attendance is requested) appeared for the first Saint Patrick's Ball which was held at the Mansion House Hotel.

The Shamrock and the harp are the enduring symbols of Irish pride. Daniel Tracey, an influential journalist at the time, encouraged his transplanted countrymen to wear the "little green leaf," which grows wild "among the flowers of our sea-guarded Isle."

"Remembering the charms it once fondly caressed, re-membering the dear ones, who round they are playing, shall wear thee this day in the land of the west."

There had been an Irish presence in New France almost from its very beginnings. A mercenary, Tadhg Cornelius O'Brennan, arrived in Montreal from France in 1659. Then, in 1672, when Louis De Buade, Comte de Frontenac was dispatched as governor, his chamberlain Pierre Lehait was in fact a Peter Leahy from County Wicklow. By the end of the 17th century at least a hundred families of Irish ancestry were living in New France. An Irish brigade served with Montcalm on the Plains of Abraham.

The first recorded celebration of St. Patrick's Day in Lower Canada was in 1765 when Miles Prentice, the former Provost-Marshal in Wolfe's Army, held a gathering in the Sun Tavern on Rue St. Jean in Quebec City.

Chapter Two

MONTREAL'S ST. PATRICK'S PARADE began as a small but rousing procession for the select few. Anyone, whether Roman Catholic or Protestant, could join. All that was required was that you be of Irish descent. Religious and political differences were off the table. In essence, for the first decade of the parade's history, the walk was a public declaration by a privileged group of prominent Irishmen who met to appreciate the liberty they enjoyed under British rule in Lower Canada. Their parade focused on ethnic moorings, and its participants fully expected the same justice for their Irish homeland where the great Irish Catholic liberator Daniel O'Connell had just launched an ultimately successful reform campaign to achieve emancipation.

In his study of Montreal's Irish community, Kevin James contends that the first St. Patrick's parades represented "the highest class and middling echelons of capital and civic power." Those who took part were conservatives united by a common commitment to British rule in North America. Over the course of the next decade, however, the working-class Irish Catholics made common cause with the French-speaking nationalists and their *patriote* movement. Inspired in part by O'Connell's activism in Ireland and spurred on in Montreal by Jocelyn Waller's newspaper, *The Canadian Spectator,* the Irish in Canada began agitating for a better deal within the British Canadian provinces.

Waller, described as being "amiable, and of virtuous character," was the son of an Irish baronet and came to Canada as a civil servant in 1817, but was removed from his duties because of his radical views. He was among the guests at the St. Patrick's dinner in 1826 where he was toasted as the "defender of Canadian rights." That dinner was hosted by *patriote* sympathizer Dr. Timothée Kimber, who supported Louis-Joseph Papineau, who was seen as the champion of French-Canadian interests. Waller's newspaper records that at least 15 toasts were made during the evening, including one to the "Irish Soldier," (the Dublin born Duke of Wellington); to the emancipation of Ireland; to Daniel O'Connell, the defender of Irish rights; and to "Irish wit and Irish conviviality." O'Connell's successful election in the 1828 Clare County by-election revived the parliamentary efforts at reform at home and were cheered by the Irish abroad.

Irish and French in Quebec were spiritually united through the Catholic Church, but, after the conquest in 1759, many of those with Irish roots became a hybrid entity being assimilated into the French-speaking Catholic majority. Waller died in 1828. His mission was taken up by another Irish-born firebrand, Daniel Tracey who had begun publishing the *Irish Vindicator and Canada General Advertiser,* an organ started by the Friends of Ireland Society. If Tracey despised the British, he despised Montreal's English-speaking ruling class even more. His broadsheet was a strident voice for the Gaelic community and promoted Irish common cause with French Canadians. He attacked Orangemen as "assassins, who could think of nothing that is not dyed in the blood of Irish Catholics. Red hue attracts their devotion and the idols of their worship are the putrid and mangled and murdered bodies of the people of Ireland," he wrote. Tracey's broadsheet became the English voice for Louis-Joseph Papineau. In January 1834, Papineau's Parti Patriote drafted 92 resolutions which sought to improve the workings of the Legislative council. The document, inspired in part by both the French and American revolutions, basically demanded that council be responsible to the people it was meant to represent and not to the so-called "Château Clique" that was in charge. The Imperial Government rejected the demands, and a small but vocal number of the working-class Irish who resented domination by a British Protestant State joined their French-Canadian brethren in seething protest.

Tracey endorsed the resolutions and was arrested for libel. He was jailed for six weeks. His imprisonment made him a hero. When he was released from gaol, not only was he cheered as he walked in that year's St. Patrick's Parade, but he was also chosen as a candidate to run in a by-election in Montreal West. It was a hotly contested race between the English and the *Patriote* party which saw the Orangemen exercise their influence in Montreal for the first time. The *Gazette* warned that "Irish Roman Catholics would coalesce with French Canadians" to frustrate the Anglo ruling class. Tempers flared. On May 21, as Tracey took the lead in the vote, emotions ran high. Soldiers of the 15th Regiment were called out to quell what was deemed as an apprehended insurrection. A fight broke out among those who were voting, and the army opened fire in order to disperse the crowds.

Three people, all of them *patriote* supporters, were killed.

Tracey won the by-election by three votes but died of cholera two months later. The editor who took over *The Vindicator*, Edmund Bailey O'Callaghan, not only continued to support Papineau's campaign with his super-heated editorials but became Papineau's right hand. O'Callaghan was elected to the House of Assembly that year where he was recognized as the most spirited *patriote* in French Canada. As the colony became increasingly polarised, open rebellion became more and more apparent.

At this point Patrick Phelan, a Sulpician priest from Ballragget, Ireland, was engaged to separate his parishioners from the French-Speaking Catholic Community and promote them as a distinct English-speaking minority. The Sulpicians were worried that militant organizers of the St. Patrick's Parade had co-opted the saint's day for political ends. St. Patrick's Day always falls during the religious observance of Lent, a 40-day period between Ash Wednesday and Easter which is supposed to be marked by penitence and self-denial, not drunken revelry. Phelan insisted that the day was to be observed as a religious occasion, not as a *patriote* festival, and that it was not an excuse to get blind drunk. He set out to establish a greater episcopal authority over the parade and its organizers by starting a "Temperate Association," said to be the first of its kind in North America. Phelan was also instrumental in the decision to have a church built for the Irish.

In March of 1834, Mass was celebrated for Irish Catholics in the parish church, Notre-Dame, which had opened in 1829. "The Rev. Mr. Holmes delivered an excellent discourse to a crowded congregation, and about 80 pounds were afterwards collected in aid of finishing the interior of the church."

There were two St. Patrick's dinners, one at Swords' Hotel given by O'Callaghan for the *patriote* Irish, the other "an excellent and abundant" meal at McCabe's Hotel hosted by Michael O'Sullivan. Among the many toasts at McCabe's there was one to Ireland, "as she ought to be, great, glorious and free." They sang the loyal Irishman's Anthem, "*Up with the banner, let loyal breath fan her. She'll blaze o'er the heads of our gentlemen still. Ho, Irishmen rally from mountain and valley, around the old flagstaff on Liberty's hill.*"

The gathering at McCabe's was under Phelan's influence. It marked the founding of the St. Patrick's Society which started in opposition to the *patriote* cause. The Society's first president was John Donnellan, a horticulturalist who arrived in Montreal in 1821 to sell ornamental shrubs, Lombardy poplars, and fruit trees. The *Canadian Spectator* referred to him as "the gardener," who "took a piece of ground in some acres of this city and by his skill, taste and steady industry, and by his abstemious domestic life, has become 'the lord of the soil.'" He had started out as a *patriote* supporter but, alarmed at the radical direction the movement was taking, joined the English party "out of a desire to promote the interests of

Irishmen." Described in one account as "a true- born, true-hearted Irishman," he designed the badge for the Montreal Hibernian Benevolent Society which features "a blood-red cross on a silver field in the centre of which shall be a harp of gold." It remains the society crest used to this day.

Michael O'Sullivan and Benjamin Holmes were elected vice presidents, and Thomas Begley, the treasurer. The *patriote* Irish shunned Donnellan as a turncoat and never forgave him. In October 1834, a verse denouncing him, *John Donnellan, My Joe, John* appeared in the *Vindicator*:

> *You left our ranks in dudgeon*
> *And joined a mortal foe;[…]*
> *For the Irish have resolved, John*
> *To stick like friends together*
> *And not desert the truth, John,*
> *For you or any other.*
> *With Papineau and Nelson, John*
> *They triumphed long ago*
> *And they'll conquer with the same again*
> *John Donnellan, my Joe.*

There were two processions again in 1835—this time one led by Donnellan which included representatives of the Scots who had founded their own St. Andrew's Society, and one led by the English who had begun the St. George's Society. Accompanied by the band of the 24th Regiment, they attended Mass together where Father Phelan preached "on the various subjects, such as the house of industry, the story of St. Patrick's conversion to Christianity." According to the *Gazette*, the Protestants in attendance, "left the building speaking well of the experience," although later in the day, two Catholics in the procession were arrested for disorderly conduct. The other "unofficial" parade staged by the "*patriote*" Irish, ended up at Swords' Hotel, which had been decked out with "a rich and elegant green banner, bearing the appropriate device of an Irish harp." The "official" dinner that evening, "sumptuous in the extreme," was at the Theatre Royal which had been transformed into "an apartment of suitable dimensions and of great elegance." Women were not accepted as members of the society, and according to the *Montreal Courier*, "the daughters of Erin crowded the upper tier of boxes and with true national feeling surveyed the assembly of fathers, husbands, brothers and friends all engaged in perpetuating those associations which peculiarly belong to the land of their forefathers." Two paintings by James Duncan were placed at either end of the room, one of St. Patrick which was so well done "he seemed to be in the act of walking from the canvas." Michael O'Sullivan was at the head table decorated with "shamrocks entwined with roses and thistles," flanked by Peter McGill (St. Andrew's Society) and John Molson (St. George's Society). The wines served, according to one account, were "superior to what is generally placed on the table."

The members of the more radical Hibernians Society dined together "with a room fitted out for the occasion" at another dinner in Mr. Charles-Séraphin Rodier's House "for the exclusive purpose of venting political speeches abusive of the executive in the colony, but little was said about Ireland or Irishmen. Toasts were drunk with much fervor: 'Papineau!' and to the memory of Waller and Tracey."

Hours before the 1836 parade was to begin, the Irish contingent was again supported by "a large concourse" of members of the St. Andrew's, the St. George's, and the German societies all assembled in front of the Albion Hotel, and together "formed a most imposing and numerous procession." Prominent among those marching was William Workman, then a hardware merchant and rising real estate developer who had come to Canada in 1829.

"We are happy to say, that a more numerous, respectable, and orderly procession never was seen in the streets of Montreal," the *Gazette* reported. Another account of that year's parade mentions the Standard of Ireland, featuring a gold harp and four gold stars on a green background, being carried by the Parade Marshal flanked by soldiers "with battle-axes," and followed by Irish pipers and the band of the 32nd Royal Irish Regiment.

At the dinner that evening, toasts were offered to the King; the navy and army; and also to "Our Countryman," the Governor-in-Chief, Sir John Colborne; and the Garrison of Montreal. "The viands which graced the table, they were prepared in the best style. The evening passed with the greatest union and cordial pleasure and the company broke up at an early hour and looked forward with anticipation to the next returning anniversary."

In March of 1837, there was a low-key procession from Orr's Hotel to Notre-Dame Church "where a sermon was preached and a collection made in aid of the friends of the House of Industry." After Mass the participants walked west from Place d'Armes to McGill then south and back east along St. Paul Street to Bonsecours Chapel. As the parade made its way through the streets, "the banners of the other societies were floating from apartments in different parts of the city and were duly saluted as the body passed." But the banquet that evening was cancelled because of cholera. Organizers were, however, able to report that "the members very liberally contributed to the causes of charity."

In the spring which followed, Dr. Wolfred Nelson, a radical anglophone who supported the *patriote* cause, famously declared that the time had come "to melt down our dishes and spoons to make bullets." Nelson organized a series of protest demonstrations and in November warrants charging him and 25 others with high treason were issued. Soon afterwards, Louis-Joseph Papineau,* Edmund Bailey O'Callaghan, and a small number of Irish followers joined Nelson in the village of St. Denis where on December 4, 1837, they declared the Independence of Lower Canada. The British army moved in to crush the uprising but unprepared for military action, it ran out of ammunition and was defeated at the Battle of St. Denis.

The *patriote* victory was short lived.

The second battle, at Saint-Charles-sur-Richelieu, re-sulted in a crushing defeat for the rebels at the hands of the Royal Scots. The British army moved swiftly to put an end to the uprising in Lower Canada at Saint-Eustache. Then it laid waste to the countryside and torched the houses of the rebel leaders. Nelson fled the country but was arrested and exiled to Bermuda. He was later granted amnesty by the British and returned to Montreal where he was elected mayor in 1854. Papineau, too, was later allowed to return to his estate at Montebello. O'Callaghan, however, was condemned as a coward within the Irish community for deserting the battlefield instead of attending to the wounded and dying revolutionaries.

Following the rebellion Lord Durham was named Governor General and High Commissioner for British North America and sent to Canada to resolve "an extraordinary state of things."

Political unrest was still festering in Upper Canada in the spring of 1838 and the St. Patrick Parade that year was smaller than usual. Understandably, it was held under the watchful eye of the Royal Artillery. That evening, an entertainment *The Irish Tutor* described as a "laughable farce," was staged at the Theatre Royal.

In 1839, St. Patrick's Day was on a Sunday so the parade, led by the band of the 24th Regiment, was held on Monday, March 18. "The beautiful banners had a very imposing effect and excited the admiration of a vast concours of spectators," the *Gazette* remarked, "and the procession was frequently greeted by the cheering of their fellow citizens."

Chapter Three

WITH THE FAILURE OF THE 1837 Rebellion, Ultramontane Catholicism was able to exert its influence in Lower Canada. In effect, the Church became a parallel government. Priests railed against secular ideas. Anyone who fought for a more open, liberal society was considered a rabble rouser whose ideas were "incompatible with obedience to Church teaching." As Terrence Murphy and Roberto Perin write in the *Concise History of Christianity in Canada*, French Canadians spontaneously identified with Ultramontane thinking, "not because they were intellectually committed to the cause of reaction but because such issues reinforced their sense of a collective self."

But as Sulpician priests increasingly mobilized French Catholics in Quebec, a large segment of the Irish Catholic population began to focus its attention on the growing poverty in their homeland where a third of the country was starving. Their politics began to be informed not by local churchmen, but by Irish reformer Daniel O'Connell who had begun to mobilize Catholic Ireland with his spellbinding oratory. Catholics in Ireland could not own land, inherit property, or vote. A Catholic in Ireland could gain all the rights of a British citizen only if he renounced his faith. Famine was widespread, and a Catholic could not get something to eat unless he became a Protestant. Very few did.

By 1840, the newspapers noticed that the parade in Montreal was growing each year. The *Gazette* recorded the increasing numbers of units that took part in that year's procession. "The anniversary of Ireland's patron saint was observed with due honour this afternoon, by the St. Patrick's Society, the members of that charitable association assembled at Mr. McAuley's hotel, *New Market*, about half past eight o'clock, and walked, in procession, to the Recollect Church, and there being joined by the Christian Doctrine Society and the Montreal Catholic Temperance Association proceeded by St. James Street to the Place d'Armes, and the Parish Church where divine service was performed. The procession then reformed, and passed the banners of the German, St. George's, and St. Andrew's Society which were displayed along Notre-Dame and St. Paul Streets."

Three events in the next decade would change the dynamics of Montreal and eventually alter the concept of the parade itself: a strike by Irish workers on the Lachine Canal in 1843, the opening of St. Patrick's Church in 1847, and the subsequent arrival later that year of the Irish famine.

In January 1843, itinerant labourers from Cork and Connaught working on the expansion of the Lachine Canal went on strike for higher wages and better working conditions. By early March, hundreds of them launched protest demonstrations through the streets of Montreal. Led by a band of fife players, one procession entered the city through Notre-Dame and made its way to Place d'Armes. Representatives of the canal workers were invited into the Bank of Montreal to meet with Father Phelan and with the head cashier Benjamin Holmes, who had recently been elected president of the St. Patrick's Benevolent Society. The parade was a sombre affair, a protest demonstration during which the immigrant workers declared their loyalty to the Queen in an attempt to reach out to a broader community. "Three cheers for the Queen, long may she reign, and three cheers for old Ireland. We will Not surrender to contractors who want to live by the sweat of our brow," they chanted.

The parade snaked and looped its way into Griffintown where members of the St. Patrick's Benevolent Society collected money to help the families of those workers who had died or had been injured on the job. The St. Patrick's Society agreed to manage the money collected. *Les Mélanges Religieux was especially sympathetic to the workers, and, in an editorial suggested that working conditions had driven the employees to "satanic excess."* It was, according to Dan Horner, writing in the *Urban History Review,* "a crucial moment in identity formation for both the striking canal workers and for the Irish elite." Horner says the canal workers were at last accepted into the Irish mainstream and by those in the community "which did the heavy lifting that came with the positions of leadership and authority to which they were seeking greater access."

In June 1843, the labour dispute erupted into violence and during a riot at Beauharnois, at least eight striking workmen were killed. British troops were called in to restore order: some labourers were shot, some were cut down by sabres, and others drowned. To this day it remains the most devastating slaughter of striking workers in Canadian history.

On September 26, 1843, the seven cornerstones for St. Patrick's Church were placed and construction of "the exclusive centre of worship for the Catholics of the English language" was underway.

A collection taken for the church building fund before the 1844 parade raised 32 pounds, or about $4,000. Two weeks before the parade, Montreal became the capital of the United Canadas and residents were in a celebratory mood. St. Patrick's Day fell on a Sunday and as a result, "the parish church was crowded with the sons of the Emerald Isle and many of our other citizens. After the service the Temperance Society walked in procession from (Notre-Dame) to the Recollect Church and the order observed as well as the respectable appearance of the large assemblage of men, young and old, was pleasant to behold."

Participants followed the band of the 89th Regiment and made a circuit of Old Montreal's main streets. According to the *Gazette*, "the various flags, banners and other decorations gave the whole a very imposing effect."

There are no accounts of the 1845 parade, but a few days before the *Gazette* mentioned that the St. Patrick's Society will celebrate the national festival on Monday, March 17, by walking in procession to the church which was still under construction."

In 1846, "splendid flags and banners and the appearance

of the excellent band of the 52nd Regiment, and the Temperance Society, rendered the scene animated and attractive." The *Gazette* also reported that the parade was "orderly and well conducted and so far as we have heard, no disturbance of breach of the peace occurred during the day." But there were indications of growing tension between the younger men in the St. Patrick's Society who wanted it to be more inclusive and those traditionalists who wanted it kept strictly religious. Yet perhaps none of the parades have been more meaningful to the community or as significant as the one that began at seven in the morning outside the Recollect Church on March 17, 1847, and walked up the hill for the opening of St. Patrick's Church. Led by Marshal John Macdonald, a grand and impressive procession of 4,000 filled the church, "very lofty and well lighted by a vast quantity of long narrow windows beautifully decorated and stained, yet so as not to obscure the rays."

Bishop Ignace Bourget was in Rome, so his coadjutor, Jean Charles Prince celebrated the first "Green Mass" in the church. An account in the Sulpician archives records the day "was certainly a memorable one for the Irish of the city, the sheer size of the building evidence of their faith and determination." Three months after the church opened, famine ships carrying thousands of Irish immigrants arrived in Montreal. Many of the Irish detested the idea of living in a British colony and those who could afford to immediately left for the United States. Thousands died. Hundreds were orphaned. Those who remained alive fuelled their hatred of all things British and in time, would contribute to the

A grand procession marked the opening of
St. Patrick's Church on March 17, 1847.
Canadian Illustrated News

already fractured state of colonial government. The raw numbers paint a grim demographic picture. After 1847, the Irish presence in Canada was unavoidable. They initially occupied the lowest levels of the labour market. But unlike other European refugees, they were overwhelmingly Roman Catholic, had a power base, resented British political authority, and had a knack for political organization. But the unexpected cost of providing medical aid and welfare to the estimated 20,000 who arrived within a year put a strain on public finances. During the parade in 1848, money for the Immigrant Orphan Asylum was collected. "Many of the most esteemed citizens were present," and more people than ever before walked in procession, "and the whole passed off with the greatest order and harmony."

In June of 1848, a priest originally from Drogheda arrived from Sulpician headquarters in France and was assigned to minister to the growing number of Montreal's Irish. Rev. Patrick Dowd quickly became suspicious of the motives of some members of the St. Patrick's Society, perhaps because the society had elected as its president a rising 22-year-old lawyer, Francis Cassidy. Cassidy had grown up in Saint-Jacques-de-L'Achigan and was as much French Canadian as he was Irish. More troubling to Dowd was that Cassidy was also the secretary of the Institut Canadien which began as a French-Canadian intellectual think tank. It threatened the established order with its more nuanced approach to Ultramontane doctrine and its opposition to British domination. Cassidy opened its membership and its radical ideas to English-speaking members, including Protestants.

One week before the 1849 parade, the Legislative Assembly passed the Rebellion Losses Bill designed to compensate those who had lost property during the 1837 Rebellion. Since most of the victims were French Canadians, English-speaking Conservatives regarded the measure as a reward for treason. The 1849 parade was all but ignored in the controversy that followed, but a brief mention was made of the "Irish celebrants" who attended divine service at St. Patrick's. "On coming out they then marched through the principal streets of the city."

On April 25, a mob descended on the Parliament of the United Canadas and burned it to the ground.

Chapter Four

SAINT PATRICK'S DAY IN 1850 fell on a Sunday and in the wake of the destruction of Parliament, there was no mention that year in the paper of a street parade. But there certainly had to have been one. By the 1850s twenty per cent of Montreal's population was of Irish extraction, about 12,000 people, more than the English and Scots combined.

In the summer of 1850, a fire swept through Griffintown. Consequently, the 1851 parade was a fundraiser to help those who had been burned out of their homes. It was hailed as "a triumphant festival of a nation's joy and the ever-vivid manifestation of the faith of Ireland's children, scattered abroad, as they are over the face of the earth, yet annihilating space by their unanimous celebration of the feast of their beloved apostle."

By 1852, the crowds who took part had swelled to more than 5,000 and stretched for a mile. Watching from a second-storey window, one observer described it as "one dense mass of moving mortality." *The Herald* called it "the most numerous and respectable ever witnessed in the city." Banners flew from buildings along the route and "the appropriate badges lent additional grandeur to the scene and the whole was calculated to inspire in the Irish breast—at all times patriotic—feelings of pride in the ancient glory of the nation." Lavish dinners were held at Ryan's and O'Meara's hotels after the parade, but the biggest celebration was at St. Lawrence Hall where in a toast to Queen Victoria, Parade Marshal Alderman Thomas Ryan suggested that the Irish in Montreal had every reason to be proud of the British monarch because in 1850 she gave had given birth to a son whom she named Patrick, the Duke of Connaught. He had indeed been christened Arthur William Patrick Albert, "while there wasn't a George or an Andrew or a David in the whole royal family."

There is no record of a parade taking place in 1853 and if it did, it would have been through the ruins of the city following the great fire nine months earlier in which one third of the city was destroyed.

In June of 1853, the guarded relationship between Catholics and Protestants in Montreal was poisoned by Alexandro Gavazzi, a defrocked monk who went on to become an evangelical preacher with a mission to denounce Roman Catholicism. Preaching in Zion Church a block from St. Patrick's as he delivered an anti-Catholic tirade, a band of Catholics tried to force their way into the church and disrupt Gavazzi's service. Montreal's mayor, Charles Wilson, who was a prominent member of the St. Patrick's Society, called in the troops of the 26th Regiment. The soldiers opened fire and dozens were killed. The mayor was blamed for ordering the troops to break up the demonstration. Sectarian fury mounted.

There would be no Union Jack flying in the 1854 parade. According to the *Gazette* the day was "bright and cheering." "The procession was described as "an immense one, accompanied by three bands and a large number of banners and flags." Except the Jack. "It was seen by some as an unpleasant significance," the paper reported. For the first time, *pain beni*, loaves of bread blessed by the clergy, were distributed to those taking part.

In December 1854, a second parish for the Irish was created when St. Ann's Church opened in Griffintown as a centre of worship for the families of the Irishmen who had begun construction of the Victoria Bridge. St. Ann's would develop a proud, working-class community network that would increase the parade ranks.

In 1855, the parade was marshaled by John McDonald and two deputies on horseback. Stewards with wands, past presidents and vice presidents were followed by the chaplains and the clergy from St. Patrick's and St. Ann's. The Grand Sunburst banner brought up the rear. A dinner at O'Meara's on Place d'Armes was held after the parade. "The proceedings of the evening were characterized by the utmost good feeling and uninterrupted harmony and the social gathering did not break up until the neighbouring seminary clock warned of the approach of Sunday morning."

The appearance of harmony was deceptive, for a movement to dissolve the St. Patrick's Society was already afoot. "There were dark mutterings about the Irish and the St. Patrick's Society and other indications of religious intolerance." Even though the St. Patrick's Society described itself as a "national society," it was, in fact, a hybrid group that was frequently divided over the character of which "national" constituency it claimed to represent. Father Dowd recommended that two separate organizations be formed, one Catholic, the other Protestant, "to attend respectively to the people of their own creeds." A dispute over delegate selection for a conference in Buffalo called to consider the formation of an Irish colony in North America seems to be at the heart of the problem.

The nominations of Bernard Devlin, a 31-year-old lawyer with liberal views who had recently arrived from Roscommon, and George Clerk, a more pliable candidate, resulted in "a good deal of ill-feeling," among many of the clergy. Devlin was a crusading lawyer whose mantra—radical for the times—was "justice and equality to all classes and creeds, undue favour to none," challenged Ultramontane thinking. Father Dowd wanted a third, more conservative representative, William Patrick Bartley to attend. But members didn't appreciate the Church meddling in the delegate selection process. The divisions over the society's rules not only pitted Protestant factions against Catholics but split the Catholic community as well. From his pulpit, Father Dowd called for the dissolution of both the Young Men's St. Patrick's Association led by Devlin, and the St. Patrick's Society. "What has been the trouble, we are not informed; but there are some indications that the young men were beginning to think for themselves, and therefore must be swamped by the 'beloved laity' who are older and better drilled," suggested the *Montreal Witness*.

On January 15, Dowd brokered a meeting at O'Mears' Hotel. A spirited debate followed over whether the constitution of the St. Patrick's Society allowed the Church to interfere in its operations. In the end, by a vote of 36-21, members voted to disband the society and turn over its holdings in trust to the "clergy of St. Patrick's Church."

Both societies were dissolved and replaced by two separate organizations in order "to embrace elements in which jealous feelings would be extinguished." As the *Montreal Witness* ironically stated, "The young men gracefully laid their necks under the feet of the priests."

The new St. Patrick's Society set out three objectives: to promote harmony and goodwill among Irishmen, to render assistance whenever necessary to persons of Irish birth and their descendants, and to represent Irish interests in the city.

Now that the society was under the control of the Church, Dowd claimed that his only interest in interfering was "the welfare, respectability and happiness" of his congregation. Dowd expressed satisfaction that members could now "labour together hand and soul for the good of religion and the honour of our dear old homeland."

The Young Men's Society held a second special meeting where 19 of its members attempted to challenge Dowd's interference. They introduced a resolution which read, "belying the heated conflict which has transpired, we the members of this association cannot now separate without calling to mind the many happy hours and the social intercourse we have enjoyed together since the formation of this body. The Irish sentiment and brotherly love which have characterized us during that time will ever animate us throughout our lives."

Although the society was officially dissolved, the ecumenical spirit which animated it remained at the core of its younger membership. A Protestant newspaper, The *Witness* claimed that the younger members of the parish bowed to clerical pressure. "When the young French Canadians formed the *Institut Canadien* to think and act for themselves, the priests, as a matter of course, tried in every way to smother them, but failed. But Irish young men of this city appear to have less love of liberty or less resolution than the French."

In a letter dated February 18, Father Dowd explained that by dissolving the society, members had "the lasting gratitude of their pastors, and are regarded by them not only as an example worthy of imitation for men willing to labour together hand and soul for the good of the Church." Under Dowd's influence, the new group, The Saint Patrick's National Organization, took over management of the parade. It would become as Catholic as it was Irish, celebrated with all the piety of a Holy Day of Obligation. At the dinner after the parade in 1856, a toast to the embattled Pope Pius IX was made before the toast to the Queen. That was too much for members of the Andrew's Society, who balked at the idea of drinking a toast to the Pope. That prompted the *Montreal Witness* to complain that "Roman Catholics have, by the advice of their priests, appropriated the whole thing to themselves exclusively."

The Protestants responded by starting their own Irish Protestant Benevolent Society on April 8, 1856, and elected William Workman as its first president.

Father Dowd gained a valuable ally with the arrival in Montreal in 1857 of a newspaper publisher from the

United States, Thomas D'Arcy McGee. McGee was born in County Louth, Ireland and emigrated to Boston in 1842. Disillusioned with the United States, he eventually moved to Montreal where he started a newspaper, *The New Era*, which promoted an "extreme moderate" approach to both his Catholic faith and to politics. McGee's views would clash with those of Bernard Devlin, who by now was the commander of a volunteer rifle company. His militia was one of two that marched in the 1857 parade. The procession was led by the Prince's Brass Band, followed by another "independent" band. The Sunburst banner was carried in front of members of the St. Patrick's Society who marched three deep. Members of the Temperance Society came next, and the parade marshal and the Sarsfield Band brought up the rear. The *Gazette* congratulated its Irish brethren for "their muster, which was one of the best they had ever had in this city."

The streets for the 1858 parade were so wet and sloppy "that promenading was very unpleasant." That didn't stop the Irish from turning out with marching bands and banners. The parade began at eight in the morning when a company of volunteer rifles joined members of the St. Patrick's Society and the Temperance Association. They went to Mass together where a collection was taken up for the poor. After Mass anyone was welcome to join the procession and to hear the speeches at St. Patrick's Hall. Then the Roman Catholics went for dinner at Compain's Restaurant, "where the love of country was the order of the day."

In the spring of 1859, the procession was held to celebrate the 40th anniversary of the ordination of Pope Pius IX. The participants made a detour through Griffintown where "a bright and balmy sun and west wind drew out our fellow citizens of Irish origin to see the display made by the sons of Erin." It was later that spring that construction crews at work on the Victoria Bridge, most of them of Irish origin, uncovered "the district of death," in Pointe St. Charles where the famine Irish had been buried in mass unmarked graves a decade earlier.

On December 1, a 30-tonne black rock which had been pulled from the river was dedicated as a memorial "to preserve from desecration the remains of 6,000 immigrants who died of ship fever, A.D. 1847-48." The rock was placed on property owned by the Grand Trunk Railway. No Catholics were invited to the dedication.

Chapter Five

AT A MEETING IN NEW YORK in 1858, disgruntled Irishmen started an American-Irish Revolutionary movement with the idea of liberating Ireland from the British. Known as the Fenian Brotherhood, the Republican organization was inspired by legendary fierce Celtic warriors, *Fianna Eireann*. It quickly gained ground in the United States of America as recruits signed up to begin military training in the militia units which had sprouted up in the decade after the Mexican-American war. These men were eager to gain the necessary experience for the revolution they planned to launch "in the old land." According to Christopher Klein, the author of *When the Irish Invaded Canada*, in less than a year Fenians had infiltrated 40 U.S. military regiments and the movement gained ground in Canada.

In Montreal, a prominent building contractor, Francis Bernard MacNamee, called for the formation of an Irish military unit, ostensibly to defend Lower Canada from a Fenian threat. MacNamee had come to Canada from Cavan Ireland in 1839 and had overseen the construction of the fever sheds in 1847. He was later contracted to build a number of roads, including Mill and des Seigneurs Streets.

In 1850, Bernard Devlin was elected president of the St. Patrick's Society and helped MacNamee put together an Irish Company of "citizen soldiers" for the Prince of Wales Regiment. The regiment almost certainly had a covert Fenian agenda. While there is no evidence to prove that Devlin, who would be elected to city council, was himself a card-carrying Fenian, he was undoubtedly sympathetic to the cause. His younger brother, Owen, was certainly involved in the movement.

During the decade, Fenian sentiment infected both men who served in the Prince of Wales Regiment and who were leaders of the St. Patrick's Society. Soldiers of the 4th and 5th Company of Devlin's volunteers led the parade in 1860. The parade was delayed for about a half an hour until all the members of the various temperance societies could assemble. Once the signal was given, the band struck up "*St. Patrick's Day*," and they marched up Beaver Hall Hill to the beat of "*The Harp that Once Through Tara's Hall.*"

The Fenians had adopted as their flag an 18th-century Irish battle standard, Gal Gréine, which featured a gold sun burst on a green background. The flag was carried into St. Patrick's Church for the first time that year as a symbol of quiet Irish pride. The *Gazette* records that "the moment the parade entered the sacred edifice everything was hushed." Many in the congregation dismissed the flag as a harmless expression of support for Ireland, but its presence in the church angered one parishioner, Thomas D'Arcy McGee, who had recently been elected to the Legislative Assembly of the Province of Lower Canada. McGee vowed, as he

Bernard Devlin, the dynamic president of the St. Patrick's Society, was elected in 1850.

once put it, "to strangle" the Fenian movement, "and not be annoyed by its carcass."

On March 4, 1861, Abraham Lincoln was sworn in as the 16th President of the United States. One week later the Confederate states adopted a constitution of their own. Both sides of the border were unsettled by what the *Northern Witness* called "a war in anticipation." That year, St. Patrick's Day fell on a Sunday and was observed as a solemn religious holiday.

The previous Thursday, about 100 men attended a testimonial dinner for McGee who characteristically denounced the rising Fenian movement. "We have no right to intrude our Irish patriotism on this soil for our first duty is to the land where we live and have fixed our homes," he thundered. "There is nothing more dreadful than feuds arising from exaggerated feelings of religion and nationality. The only requisite for making Canada the happiest of homes is to rub down all sharp angles and to remove those asperities which divide the people." The following Tuesday, 190 young performers staged a benefit concert for the Protestant Benevolent Society in Nordheimer's Music Hall.

In April, Confederates attacked Fort Sumter and the United States was plunged into a civil war. The *Gazette* was the first to voice its editorial support for the South. The newspaper condemned the practice of slavery but reasoned that "practically we are all slaves more or less. What have we to do with the institution of slavery in the United States? It does not affect us."

Once Britain declared its neutrality in the conflict, Montreal became the centre for an expat community of southerners and a hotbed of growing Fenian activity. It is estimated that 150,000 Irish immigrants participated in the Civil War, 30,000 of them in the Confederate army. During the hostilities, the family of confederate President Jefferson Davis sought refuge in Montreal. The Donegana Hotel at the corner of Notre-Dame and Bonsecours became the headquarters for confederate agents. To complicate mat-ters, after the Union navy forcibly boarded a British ship, *Trent*, in neutral waters and seized confederate agents heading for London, there was widespread trepidation that Lincoln would wage war on two fronts, invade British North American provinces, and annex the Canadas.

As a consequence, a heavy Canadian military presence was in evidence at the St. Patrick's Parade in 1862. In spite of a blizzard the day before, several companies from the Prince of Wales Regiment and various other bodies formed in procession. First came a company of the Foot Artillery headed by Hardy's band, next companies, the 4th and 5th Battalions of the Prince of Wales Rifles Regiment, followed by St. Anne's band and the home company. "Members of the St. Patrick's Society in full regalia brought up the rear. The procession was very long, and large numbers assembled along the line of march."

Volunteer battalions were again present in "immense numbers" at the parade in 1863. Marcus Dougherty, a rising Montreal lawyer who had been raised in Vermont, was grand marshal. "Several of the volunteer battalions attended in uniform, and without arms, many of the members of which belong to other denominations. This courtesy, will we understand, be reciprocated by the Roman Catholic volunteers on the respective anniversaries of the English and Scotch volunteers?"

During this period, the Fenian movement in Montreal operated under the auspices of the Hibernian Benevolent Society, which had been founded after the Toronto riots. (Not to be confused with the Irish Protestant Benevolent Society that began in Montreal in 1856). The *Toronto Globe* estimated that there were 1,200 Fenians in Montreal. D'Arcy McGee had no accurate idea of their numbers, and suggested there were no more than 300. It was impossible to say how many subscribed to the ideology and to what degree. They operated in the shadows and gauging the depth of their resolve was elusive. "I have never known an enemy so subtle, so hard to trace, so irrational, and therefore, so hard to combat," he said. Whatever their numbers, a Roman Catholic priest Patrick Fitzgerald denounced the movement in his sermon during the Mass that year. "Keep aloof from secret societies. Desecrate not the name of Him we venerate by giving His name to such societies," Fitzgerald warned. "There must be no secret societies among Irishmen. The voice of Patrick must be heard united."

After Mass, the congregants left the church and walked east along St. Antoine to St. Denis, up the hill south to Place d'Armes, then west along Notre-Dame to McGill, up McGill to St. Jacques, then back to Place d'Armes where it broke up.

In 1864, the streets were alive with spectators and the music of the various bands playing Irish airs. Their banners and regalia "glancing in the sun" brightened the effect of an emerald city as John Wait McGauvran, the owner of several sawmills who represented St. Anne's Ward on city council, led the parade on horseback, the first time a Grand Marshal was mounted for the occasion. "Again, this national festival beloved of all time by Irishmen has once more come round to us and perhaps never more auspiciously. We believe such a beautiful morning would have pleased St. Patrick himself, and if he could only have seen such a long and imposing procession in his honour, with such a profusion of splendid flags, banners, music and other accessories, he would doubtless have been still more delighted," the *Gazette* reported.

McGauvran was back again on horseback the following year, this time riding through a miserable mix of rain and snow. "Yesterday once more the festival beloved of all true Irishmen came around again to us, but as we heard a spectator remark, 'Never was such a St. Patrick Day seen in America.' The weather indeed seemed to be holding a sort of Donnybrook Fair on its own. Wet, sloppy roads are generally one of the attributes of St. Patrick's Day, but there is generally bright sunshine overhead and not blinding sleet."

The 1865 parade was held to raise money to build a great community hall for the Irish on the west side of Victoria Square as a place where "the immigrant might receive the advice of his countrymen and the care and consolation of his church." The Hibernian Society, now under the control of Fenian interests, organized a dinner at the Exchange Hotel with speeches that launched a no-hold barred attack and called for the destruction of Britain. The program included a parody of a British patriotic song:"*Britannia,*

curse of the ocean. The scourge of the brave and the free."
A "slight disturbance" during the 1864 parade caused "a
little excitement" when "some carter [...] apparently got
somewhat roughly handled" when he "attempt[ed] to pass
down St. James street with his sleigh."

The Civil War in the United States was almost at an
end when a victorious President Lincoln was inaugurated
for his second term on March 4, 1865. Following the
Confederate surrender at Appomattox, Fenians who had
been toughened in both armies turned their attention to
more pressing matters. They chose as their "Secretary of
War," a hot-tempered Irish patriot, "Fighting Tom Sweeny,"
who had been a high-profile hero in the Union Army. Bonds
to finance weapons for the Fenian cause in Ireland began
be-ing sold in Montreal by a prominent building contractor,
and a leading member of the St. Patrick's Society, Francis B.
McNamee, promoted their sale.

Montreal was thick with Fenians and with ragtag
confederates in 1866 when James McShane, a prominent
stockbroker and livestock exporter, led the parade. The
parade route that year was decorated with arches of
evergreens and banners, and even though it was a "dis-
agreeable cold day," a large crowd was on hand. McShane
marched with "utter disregard of the serious dangers ped-
estrians encounter given the hazardous condition of the
streets." "The predominating colour was green," observed
the *Gazette*. "It took the form of banners and cropped out
in tufts of shamrocks from cap fronts, button holes and
so forth." After the parade broke up, an "immense throng"

gathered in front of Nordheimer's Hall to hear speakers, one after another, warn against a Fenian rebellion.

The talk of civil war in Ireland was denounced by one visiting priest by the name of Gardner. "Such a war would bring Irishman against Irishman in a deadly conflict," he said. "The true interests of Canada lie in the way of peaceful industry and reciprocal commerce."

That spring, as talks to create a United British Canada were making headway with the colonial office in London, McGee, too, continued his furious attacks on the Fenian movement which irritated many of his constituents, including his political opponent, Bernard Devlin.

In spite of McGee's enthusiasm, Roman Catholics in Quebec generally were for the most part lukewarm to the idea of a confederation in which Protestants got guarantees for their minority in Quebec, while at the same time the founders refused to grant the same concessions to the Irish and French-speaking Roman Catholic minorities outside of Quebec.

Things came to a head on February 17, 1866, when the British government suspended Habeus Corpus in Ireland and rounded up Irish Americans suspected of being Fenians. In retaliation, the Fenian "War Secretary" vowed to conquer Canada. A bounty was placed on McGee's head and "before the summer sun kissed the hilltops of Ireland," Sweeny vowed to take McGee and John A. Macdonald hostage. With the Civil War now over, Fenian operatives were able to buy surplus munitions and the weapons were distributed to locations along the Canadian border. Even more troubling to the locals, a significant number of Irish recruits on the

Montreal police force refused to swear an oath of allegiance to the Queen. Canadian intelligence, headed by spymaster Gilbert McMicken, prepared for Fenian attacks from St. Alban's and Buffalo.

On March 7, John A. Macdonald called out 10,000 volunteers for active duty. James McShane was among the first to sign up. In Montreal, after a cache of arms was found in a basement on St. James Street, the Hibernian Benevolent Society was instructed to cancel the parade. But the society refused to buy into the panic. The *Gazette,* too, seemed skeptical that such a threat would be carried out. "There is much talk of St. Patrick's Day being fixed upon for the Fenian invasion. But, we do not believe this. Fenians are not fools, whatever their followers may be. And they would not tell beforehand the precise manner in which they would strike a blow," the paper reasoned in an editorial, adding for good measure, that "marching, given the present state of the roads is all but impossible." McGee was fearless. Giving what was described as a "spirit stirring oration," to the St. Patrick's Society, McGee estimated there were 300,000 Irish Catholics and 378,000 Irish Protestants in Canada.

"We unite with our Irish Protestant brethren who are as good Irishmen as we are, except for their religion," McGee joked. "I have observed this day's proceedings with great satisfaction, for they prove to all the world that not one man among you is willing to place himself outside the pale of the constitution. Wicked men have dared to say that this great, industrious body of people would not be found true to the city and to the country. I tell you, the honest man who makes this assertion has a weak case and the dishonest man who makes it is a wicked scoundrel. There is no stigma of sedition in our ranks." Even Bernard Devlin assured the crowd that "no matter what transpired, St. Patrick's Day would be kept up."

Not only did the 1866 parade go ahead but the Governor General of British North America, Viscount Monck of Ballytrammon, Wexford took the salute as the parade passed by. Sporting the badge of the St. Patrick's Society in his lapel, Monck described the parade as "a protest against the design and principles of wicked men who would disgrace the name of Irishmen."

The loudest cheers were for Bernard Devlin, however, not for McGee. But as one French-language newspaper reported, "ce qu'il y a eu de remarquable dans cette célébration ça été le calme et la dignité avec lesquels tout s'est passé." In June 1866, the Fenians launched what was to have been a three-pronged attack on Canada with the goal of capturing Quebec and making it the seat of the Irish Republic in exile. One unit of about 800 men successfully made its way to the Niagara Peninsula and won a battle at Ridgeway, Ontario. But the offensive was short-lived, and the Fenians retreated when British soldiers aided by the U.S. Army thwarted any further Fenian offensives.

The St. Patrick's Parade in Montreal on March 18, 1867, was a protest rally against Bishop Bourget's decision to turn St. Patrick's into a French-speaking parish church. McGee went to Rome to appeal the decision to the Pope and on the same trip was in London putting the finishing touches on the articles of Canadian Confederation. In Montreal, the morning was "beautifully fine," as the number of participants "far ahead of anything in previous years," began their walk in Griffintown and made their way to St. Patrick's for High Mass. After the service, a crowd of more than 6,000 then made its way to Place d'Armes where Parade Marshal Joseph Cloran laid the cornerstone for St. Patrick's Hall, a proposed four-storey building "as spacious as a cathedral," whose design was inspired by Cormac Chapel in Tipperary. When completed, the building was to have shops on the ground floor, a library, billiard room, and committee rooms on the second floor, and a grand auditorium 134 feet long and 94 feet wide, the largest in North America, decorated in green and gold on the third and fourth floors. Bernard Devlin boasted that when the hall was finished, it would serve as The Parliament for "The Irish national government of the people." The event was marred by a "loud and long disturbance," sparked by a heckler in the crowd who shouted "You are all a bunch of fools," and by an accident in which a young man by the name of Jones tripped and fell and cracked his skull on some stone steps. To the superstitious Irish, a cornerstone laid in blood could only be a bad omen. After the ceremony, "banners and regalia, many of them new and rich," were drawn through the streets in horse-drawn sleighs through several triumphal arches fashioned from evergreens. But Mayor Starnes told the crowd they were not here to talk politics. "Those who accuse the Irish of our city of being disloyal commit a falsehood. All the Irish want is fair play."

On March 18, 1867, a crowd of more than 6,000 made its way to Place d'Armes where Parade Marshal Joseph Cloran laid the cornerstone for St. Patrick's Hall.

On March 29, 1867, Canada was proclaimed a Dominion. In the first federal election held that summer, McGee's relentless attacks on the Fenians had alienated him from half of his constituents. He came within a hair's breadth with 197 votes of being defeated by Bernard Devlin (2,675, 2,478). When Sir John A. Macdonald named his first cabinet, McGee was not included. He had become a political liability, especially to Macdonald's Ontario supporters. Macdonald's wife, Agnes confided to her diary that there was still "a painfully rebellious feeling among the Irish in our country."

That sentiment was fuelled by the shooting in Montreal

of a Roman Catholic coachman, Felix Prior, by John Burrows, a Protestant merchant. Burrows claimed that Prior was attempting to break into his house when he was shot and killed. He was never charged for the crime. But the St. Patrick's Society believed the killing was religiously motivated. McGee made a number of speeches in which he blamed the Fenians in the society for creating discord and division.

And he called for an end to the St. Patrick's parades.

As a newly minted Member of Parliament, McGee swore an oath of allegiance to the Queen. As a result, on January 27, 1868, the St. Patrick's Society expelled him from its ranks. Six weeks later, McGee was in Ottawa for St. Patrick's Day where he was honoured at a banquet. In Montreal, the newly elected mayor, William Workman, led the march through dense fog from Victoria Square under triumphal arches through to St. Patrick's where a Mass by Joseph Haydn was sung.

Bernard Devlin, who had engineered McGee's expulsion from the St. Patrick's Society, defiantly unfurled the Sunburst banner in the church near McGee's pew. D'Arcy McGee would never see Montreal again. He was assassinated on April 7, the victim of an apparent Fenian conspiracy. As Slattery wrote, "Canadians were seized with a sense of panic, a collective psychosis caused by the fear of the unknown."

More than 15,000 followed McGee's coffin through the streets of Montreal on what would have been his 43rd birthday. James Patrick Whelan was found guilty on circumstantial evidence of being the assassin and executed in 1869. Whelan's widow, Bridget, believed her husband to have been railroaded to the gallows and displayed his picture in a black-bordered wreath outside her boarding house along the parade route every year until her death in 1904.

Joseph Cloran was grand marshal in 1869, on a fine and frosty morning. "Again this anniversary returns to its appointed round," The *Gazette* remarked. "The associations of the day are so well known like those of most other national anniversaries that it is unnecessary to dwell upon them." A thousand people or more turned out that blustery evening for a concert in St. Patrick's Hall when the roof of the building collapsed. "The evening was moving through its happy paces. The concert having concluded, the chairs were removed and dancing had begun. Suddenly there was a sound "like the firing of a cannon overhead," followed five minutes later by three more reports in rapid succession. According to newspaper accounts the dancers went streaming for the exits, some calmly, others less so. "Some gallants rushed out, leaving their ladies to follow as best they could."

The roof consisted of boiler plates riveted together and supported by girders. Many people blamed the weight of snow on the roof for the collapse. Some pointed to vibrations caused by the dancing. One letter-writer to the *Gazette* argued confidently that strong winds had set up a chain reaction causing the plates to split apart, one after the other. A committee finally determined repeated freezing and thawing had fatally weakened the girders. The debris was cleared away and the hall restored. Wooden beams were used to support the roof, not iron girders and soon the building was as busy as ever.

Chapter Six

"Notwithstanding the heavy snowstorm which fell dur-ing the whole of St. Patrick's Day, the Irishmen of Montreal had their yearly march as usual," the *Gazette* dutifully reported in 1870. "The procession formed shortly after eight o'clock in front of St. Patrick's Church where Mass was celebrated and a sermon preached by the Rev. Mr. O'Brien of Brockville. After the conclusion of the service, the procession reformed and with Michael Marlow as Grand Marshal, it marched up de Bleury Street along which arches had been erected, east along St. Catherine Street, down St. Lawrence Main to Craig, where an arch bearing the names of British Prime Minister Gladstone and John Bright who had helped shape Irish land reforms, to St. Patrick's Hall."

A cold, wet rain in 1871 prompted Michael Bernard Buckley, a visiting priest in Montreal to raise money for Cork Cathedral to lament, "Oh Holy Saint Patrick, what did I ever do that you should treat me so?" after he walked three miles through potholes filled with icy water. "It was a grand procession. The music was excellent, the spectators and the gazers enjoyed it as it moved along. I asked if the procession gave offense to any party. All classes liked it and would be disappointed if it did not take place," he wrote. Parade Marshal Bernard Devlin was flanked by Mayor Coursal and Alderman Ryan as large crowds collected on the way. According to the *Star,* "in spite of the rain and miserable weather, the procession passed off in the most satisfactory manner."

No one knows exactly what set off the ensuing brou-haha but after the event, Father Dowd decided the parade had become "a nuisance," and the annual ball had become "dangerous, extravagant and an immoral public entertain-ment." Gleaning the papers of the day, it would seem that Dowd objected to the way the respective societies had lined themselves up for the parade, specifically the St. Patrick's Society which led the parade. In Dowd's view, the society "had no connection with the church," and therefore should have brought up the rear. In truth, Dowd needed money to pay for St. Bridget's Refuge which was under construction, and thought money spent on the parade and the ball might be better allocated to charity. The *Montreal True Witness and Catholic Chronicle* agreed with him. "Instead of trolling the streets with trumpery flags, banners and other gee gaws, we should banish all such mischievous tomfooleries." A letter to the *Montreal Star* similarly demanded that the event be abolished. "We would venture to say St. Patrick would much prefer to see the annual proceeds of all St. Patrick's pots and St. Patrick's processions devoted to Catholic charities rather than squandered on bad taste." Even through Dowd prohibited his congregation from taking part in what he called "the unauthorized and false" parade, his bishop, Ignace Bourget, over-ruled him and allowed the 1872 procession to go ahead.

The *Star* suggested that Dowd's motive "springs from a spirit of domination which would subjugate the people and take from them their most cherished rights." The parade went ahead without Dowd's approval, staged under the auspices of the St. Patrick's Benevolent Society. Decorations were not as elaborate as in previous years, but four bands played, and Mayor Charles-Joseph Coursol participated. In a sermon the following Palm Sunday, March 24, Dowd dressed down those who walked and complained that the day after the parade, "71 Irishmen appeared in court to answer to a charge of intoxication." Even as he spoke, a number of men in the congregation walked out of church in protest. At a testimonial dinner later attended by 50 of Dowd's supporters who gave him $2000 to pay off the mortgage on St. Bridget's, Dowd mellowed. The priest said he really had no objections to the parade going ahead next year and blamed the "Protestant Press" for inflaming the situation.

Early in the morning of Oct. 2, 1872, St. Patrick's Hall was engulfed in flames after a fire in a shoe factory next door spread. Destroyed in the fire were the archives and all records of previous parades. "Even had the hoses done their job, however, it's unlikely the building could have been saved, and by the break of day it was a smoldering ruin. Again, there were no deaths, nor any injuries to speak of."

The burned-out ruins of the hall were still standing in March of 1873 as the mustering point for "the whole of Ireland in Montreal" who gathered for the parade. William Hingston, a leading physician, was put in charge of the fundraising effort to have the hall rebuilt, but there

Father Dowd decided the parade had become "a nuisance," but he was over-ruled by Bishop Ignace Bourget, who allowed the 1872 parade to proceed.

wasn't enough money collected, so the hall was sold. Two calamities less than four years apart were enough. Perhaps lest fate be tempted further, St. Patrick's Hall was not rebuilt. By 1875, two new buildings had risen on the site. They're still there, though now incorporated into the International Trade Centre.

There was a downpour during the 1873 parade, and a carriage drawn by six horses had been reserved for Francis Cassidy, who had just been elected mayor. But Cassidy and the parade Marshal John O'Reilly chose to walk "through puddles of mire and pools of water." O'Reilly was a celebrated Fenian who had been arrested for his subversive activities and sent to a penal colony in Australia. He escaped and settled in Boston. "All of Griffintown was out in gay attire, flags waved from humble homes," and so many ceremonial arches had been put up in the neighbourhood that the president of the St. Patrick's Society suggested that Griffintown be renamed 'The City of Arches.'

It rained and the streets were slippery again with mud for the 1874 parade marshaled by Joseph Cloran. According to the *Star,* the stormy weather "made percussionists and spectators wish that they were comfortably ensconced in their houses." There wasn't much decoration on the parade route, "the only one of any pretension being at Mr. Tansey's Craig Street where a handsome string of Irish, French, English and American flags, including a very handsome emblem of Home Rule was suspended across the street."

St. Patrick's Day in 1875 fell on a Wednesday which may account for why the turnout that year was smaller than usual. "Usually marshals hurrying in every direction, banners flying and bands playing are the features of the day. Yesterday there were not so many of those signs," the *Gazette* reported. But there was a parade again marshalled by Joseph Cloran. "Everything was conducted decorously and the whole proceedings finished without incident. The only drawback was the state of the roads, which owing to the mildness of the weather were very slushy."

Later that year, a meeting to organize a Lodge of Orange Young Britons attended by about fifty people was held on July 27, 1875. It was encouraged by a Methodist minister, Leonard Gaetz, who insisted a Lodge in Montreal was needed "to meet a want which has long been the weakness of Protestant action. It involves the entire question of whether we have the right to hold conscientious convictions of our own in this Catholic city." It would prove to be an incendiary idea in a city in which Protestants were outnumbered by Roman Catholics 5 to 1. While Orangemen in Quebec were small in numbers, they exerted a significant influence in Ontario. With a foothold in Montreal, "a somewhat uneasy feeling prevailed, and trouble was feared by many," when plans for an Orange parade in 1876 were announced.

The Victoria Silver Cornet band played Irish airs outside St. Ann's Church even before the St. Patrick's Parade began on March 17, 1876: "people stretched their necks to get a look at the new gold chain of office" worn by the Society's president, Bernard Devlin. Flags flew from the towers of Notre-Dame, houses were decorated with evergreens, and ceremonial arches were erected along the parade route to St.

Patrick's Church. In July, more than a hundred policemen were called out for the Orange Parade, Montreal's first open celebration of the Battle of the Boyne. The police "kept spectators moving along and by this means prevented any large assembly to congregate together." However, when the parade ended, "Orange rowdies" goaded by Charles Chiniquy, who preached that Irish Catholics wanted the Pope to take control of Canada, smashed windows of the Lomas Hotel in Pointe St. Charles.

Eight men were arrested.

The following year, in sharp contrast, the *Montreal Star* was able to report "a marked absence of drunkenness and no contretemps occurred to mar the general pleasure" during the 1877 St. Patrick's Day Parade. "The only drawback was the intense cold from which many suffered severely."

That year, 200 members of a provocative new religious movement, the Irish-Catholic Union made an appearance in the parade that was marshaled by Alderman Patrick Kennedy. The union was a political organization designed to advance a Roman Catholic agenda in politics and promote Irish nationalism.

That evening a "monster attendance" was reported at the St. Patrick's concert in Mechanics Hall. But the reviews for the entertainment were scathing. Kitty Harrington's rendition of "Dear Little Shamrock" was dismissed as "sadly lacking in musical taste and culture," and Jack O'Brien "failed completely," in his attempt to sing "Let Me Like a Soldier Fall."

The Orange Parade in 1877 went ahead again in July, this time with catastrophic consequences. On July 12, Thomas

Lett Hackett, a 22-year-old Orangeman on his way home from church was shot and killed near Victoria Square. He was armed with a pistol, and the circumstances surrounding his death are suspect. The Orange Young Britons claimed he was murdered by Catholics and Protestants made a martyr out of him. The Irish-Catholic Union deplored the killing and advised its members not to disrupt Hackett's funeral procession. Mayor Beaudry declared the Orange Association illegal in Montreal. When the Orangemen vowed to parade again, Beaudry called out the militia and had 60 of its organizers arrested. In retaliation, the City of Toronto, widely known as "The Belfast of Canada" banned all further St. Patrick's Day parades in that city.

On July 12, 1877, Thomas Hackett was shot and killed.

The Orange Order in Buffalo, New York then threatened to march on Montreal with an army 20,000 strong unless all St. Patrick's Day parades in Canada be prohibited by law. In a series of letters to the *Times of London*, Sir Francis Hincks, the retired Canadian finance minister and a former prime minister of the United Canadas denounced "any foreigner who dared to pollute the soil of Canada, be they Orangemen or Fenians. They must be met at the frontier and dealt with summarily." Hincks was a Presbyterian who argued that "common sense and Christian charity," allowed the St. Patrick's Parade to take place. "It would be an unwise course to agitate for a law on the subject," he wrote. "It is the imperative duty of loyal men to obey the law, but Orangemen have not obeyed any law prohibiting them to march in procession with banners and badges." Montreal's St. Patrick's Day festivities "did not give annoyance to the great majority of Protestants in the city," he continued, "but I can readily conceive that to Orangemen and those who sympathize with their views, it is vexacious that the processions of Roman Catholics are not prohibited by law."

As a result of the growing sectarian tension, the directors of the St. Patrick's Society were under pressure to cancel the 1878 parade. By fortunate circumstance, fate intervened. The embattled Pope Pius IX who had been "held prisoner of the Vatican," during the Italian unification wars died in February. The Pope's death gave the Irish National Societies the excuse they needed to declare a period of mourning.

The parade that year was officially cancelled.

"The action taken in having determined to sacrifice the

pleasure of the procession in memory of the late pontiff militated to prevent the flow of enthusiasm generally apparent on St. Patrick's Day. Usually Marshals hurrying in every direction, banners flying and bands playing are the feature of the day. Yesterday there were not so many of these signs," The *Gazette* reported. It was a Sunday and the streets were crowded with church-goers, rosaries in hand, and "all or nearly all wore bunches of shamrocks," as they made their way to St. Patrick's. A brass band marched down de Bleury to the Gesù where members of the Saint-Jean-Baptiste Society attended Mass in honour of Ireland's patron.

Even though the parade had been cancelled, an estimated 3,000 members of the Irish-Catholic Union took to the streets after Mass with the designated parade marshal, Edward Coyle, a native of County Longford, Ireland. The *Star* reported that "Deprived of much of its outward pomp and grandeur by the National Societies abandoning their usual parade out of respect for *pio nono*, when compared to the large and imposing demonstrations that usually occur here in honour of St. Patrick, the display (this year) was meagre in the extreme."

Because the St. Patrick parade had been banned in Toronto, a trainload of Irish Catholics from the Ontario capital arrived to take part in the 1879 observance. Snow "spread a beautiful white carpet on the frozen, dirty roads," as Alderman Patrick Kennedy, president of the police commission filled the marshal's role. The parade route was decorated with "an endless display of banners," and a magnificent twin-towered ceremonial arch was erected on St. Joseph Street, with the

Union Jack flying from one tower and the French tricolour billowing from the other. In niches in the tower were statues of the Maid of Erin resting on a harp, above her the papal arms, and in the other niche, a statue of St. Patrick.

Bernard Devlin, who had been a fixture at the parade for three decades, was conspicuous by his absence. He had gone to Colorado for tuberculosis treatment where he died on February 7, 1880. His body was returned to Montreal for burial on February 16, and his body lay in state for three days at St. Lawrence Hall. His funeral procession to Notre-Dame-des-Neiges Cemetery was bigger than any parade.

Chapter Seven

As THE CITY GREW, St. Patrick's Parish was no longer the only Irish-Catholic parish on the island. By the 1880s, there were seven each with their own agenda, St. Ann's, St. Gabriel's, St. Bridget's, St. Mary's, St. Peter's, St. Joseph's, and St. Anthony's, one church for about every 600 Irish-Catholic families.

The decade began with a famine in Western Ireland. The 1880 procession was another muted, prayer-filled affair held to collect money for those starving in the old country. Representatives of four Irish societies and 800 boys from the Christian Brothers School gathered for Mass at St. Patrick's. "The Irish of Montreal did honour their patron, if not in so demonstrative a manner as on some previous occasions, with as much enthusiasm," noted the *Gazette*. Bishop Fabre celebrated Mass as a hundred-voice choir, (70 boy sopranos and 30 bass and tenors), sang a six-tone Mass "sweet and soothingly." Even though the church was filled to overflowing, one visitor noted that "The present assembly, vast as it is, represents a mite of all who are under the burning influence of St. Patrick."

Following the Mass at St. Patrick's, Grand Marshal

Bernard McNamee led everyone to St. Bridget's Church near the Jacques Cartier Bridge for another Mass and ben-ediction. The day ended with a concert of Irish airs at Nordheimer's Hall.

Later that year, McNamee was re-elected president of the St. Patrick's Society, but shortly after his election he was accused of buying the votes by bribing two thirds of the membership for its support. He was also rumoured to be a double agent, working for the Canadian government as a spy, and at the same time supplying Fenians with sensitive information. By then his antics had soured much of the membership. McNamee was forced to resign. He was replaced by Patrick Kennedy, "a son of Tipperary," who was president of the Montreal Police Commission.

As McNamee walked in the 1881 parade which was "celebrated with an éclat possibly surpassing that of any previous year," someone on the roof of a building on McGill St. threw bullets at him. Denis Perrault was arrested and charged with aggravated assault. MacNamee was unscathed in the attack, but a priest walking beside him was injured. Later that evening, McNamee was honored by his supporters at a testimonial banquet in St. Lawrence Hall in appreciation of his "well spent life." He was given an oil painting of himself and in accepting it, said, "[I am] an Irishman not ashamed of my country, only ashamed of the unjust laws by which she is oppressed and by the wretchedness under which she groans."

March 17, 1882, dawned bright and sunny but it was a bitter cold day. Nevertheless, according to the *Star,* by 8:30 that morning the streets were thronged with bystanders, "all anxious to obtain the best point for viewing the procession. Good humour was the order of the day, nothing could be heard but music and laughter."

A dozen bands blared and Marshal Alderman Kennedy rode with the Montreal Hackmen's Union, "all mounted with triple badges of a violet hue clasped with a gold maple leaf on their breasts."

The parade in 1883 was held on the heels of a wildly successful "*mini-carème*" winter carnival which had been held that year for the first time. Designed to promote the city as a winter tourist destination, it featured a magnificent castle made of ice "with towers and caves of shimmering light" as the carnival's main attraction. Perhaps infused with the energy of the successful winter festivities, Alderman Kennedy again marshalled a high-spirited crowd through beautifully decorated ceremonial arches. "In spite of the un-promising weather, large crowds of people wearing sham-rocks and green ribbons thronged the streets at an early hour," reported the *Gazette*. The streets weren't as crowded as usual, but "the procession was quite gay." As the parade made its way through Victoria Square, however, "guns were fired and several people were injured, one man severely wounded 'by a missile fired, it is supposed from an air gun. Such conduct is cowardly, and the perpetrators, if captured, should be severely punished.'"

After the parade, an overflow crowd packed the The-atre Royal for the Young Irishmen's Concert, "the pieces exceptionally well selected and the performances all that could be desired."

Alderman Patrick Kennedy advanced the parade's
Roman Catholic agenda.

A sudden and unexpected snowstorm on St. Patrick's Day in 1884 delayed the start of the parade, but Grand Marshal Kennedy weathered the storm, riding a splendid horse. However, the 200 members of the Hackmen's Union who were supposed to follow behind on horseback didn't show up because of the wretched conditions. "The Daniel O'Connell banner followed, drawn by four spirited greys. Behind this was the fife and drum band of the 6th Fusiliers." An arch "set off with appropriate mottos and famed pictures of distinguished Irishmen," was built at the corner of Craig and Panet. The parade was also memorable because after an absence of several years, Protestants again took part in the procession. "Prejudice was dying out and intelligence was taking its place," remarked Dennis Barry, a prominent lawyer who addressed the crowds. "A sure sign that Protestant and Catholic would one day walk arm and arm as they had done in days gone by."

A smallpox epidemic in the spring of 1885 claimed 6,000 lives but in spite of some misgivings, the parade went ahead. Marshal Kennedy and Mayor Honoré Beaugrand, wearing his sparkling chain of office, contributed to what was described as "the pomp and glitter of a brilliant pageant." The bishop of Montreal, Edouard-Charles Fabre, was joined at St. Patrick's for Mass by Toronto's auxiliary bishop Timothy O'Mahony. An Irish harp in the sanctuary was "larmed in lines of living fire." For the first time, a contingent of the St. Ann's Young Men's Society, the first parochial athletic and cultural association of its kind in North America, was represented in the parade. Started by Edward Strubbe, a dynamic Redemptorist priest, as "a breeding place of genius, a distributing centre for talent, and a starting point of energetic Catholicism for Irish youth," Strubbe and the society would assert their influence on the parade for years to come.

Nicholas Flood Davin, the publisher of one of the leading newspapers in the Northwest Territories, the *Regina Leader*, was also in attendance. Davin's duties as secretary of the Royal Commission on Chinese Immigration had brought him to Montreal. In a speech after the parade in Nordheimer's Hall, Davin mounted a vigorous and eloquent attack on the relationship between the Empire and Ireland, and the divisions of race and religion which threatened to explode in the Northwest. He proudly pointed out that "there was hardly a stone in Canada in which there was not the mark of an Irish chisel." The first duty of Irishmen he maintained was to Canada. "Nothing could be more base than to disturb Canada. I don't think I will ever be a saint, but I have one thing in common with St. Patrick," he said. "I love putting my heel on snakes."

Ten days after Davin's speech, twelve members of the Northwest Mounted Police force on their way with provisions to Fort Carlton were massacred by Metis forces at Duck Lake, sparking the Riel uprising. For the next six months, Davin's newspaper became a journal of national importance with its firsthand accounts of the prairie revolt. By the time Riel was hanged in November, the smallpox epidemic in Montreal which was over.

The archbishop of St. Boniface, Manitoba, Alexandre-

Antonin Taché, was honoured at the parade in 1886 with a procession at least a half a mile long. "The streets were profusely decorated with flags, bunting, or any green material which serves to impress the Irishmen's heart and remind him of that spot so dear to his heart."

In 1887, Father Dowd observed his golden jubilee as a priest and led the contingent of clergy in that year's parade. Edward Ryan was Marshal-in Chief. More than 500 children from St. Mary's parish, including 50 boys all with green sashes, rode in a sleigh drawn by four horses. Because it was St. Patrick's Day, all "prisoners of Irish extraction" had their cases in recorder's court dismissed by the judge. It snowed a little, but the streets were in good marching order until after the parade ended. It appears that some local merchants saw the advantage of commercial advertising during the parade. "The streets were very clean and walking good, but the streets were not clean for very long," complained one person in a letter to the *Gazette*, "Everywhere one went they were littered with flaming green handbills distributed by Sharp's Balsam Company."

That evening, a production of *Robert Emmett* was staged, a wrenching drama about the Irish nationalist who was hanged in 1803 for planning, with the support of the French, a rebellion against British rule.

In 1888, the premier of Quebec, Honoré Mercier accompanied by his Minister of Agriculture and Public Works, the "People's Jimmy, James McShane, a future mayor of Montreal, was the first premier to walk "under cold and clear bright sunny skies" in the parade. A harpist who played Irish airs rode in an authentic Irish jaunting cart which appeared for the first time. Large horse-drawn sleighs followed, and St. Patrick's Church was decorated on a grander scale than usual with "embroidered banners and festoons of green silk placed at all available points, the effect being very striking."

St. Patrick's Day in 1889 fell on a Sunday, so the parade was held the following Monday. Parade Marshal John Dwyer walked through the rain with Rev. James A. McCallen, a Sulpician priest from Baltimore who had recently been recruited to assist Fr. Dowd at St. Patrick's. McCallen walked with the gold-headed cane which had been given to him upon his arrival in recognition of his work with the Temperance Society and for his "zeal for ceremonies and attentive care in training choirboys." Mass at St. Patrick's was conducted with "more pomp and magnificence than usual," to welcome Archbishop Fabre, who had just returned from Rome. By all accounts, however, the best show in the procession was made by the 150 men in top hats, members of the St. Ann's Young Men's Society as well as "the three sleighs filled with children from St. Gabriel's school."

Chapter Eight

THE SOMEWHAT STAID and religiously ordered St. Patrick's processions could not by themselves satisfy the overwhelming expression of patriotic Irish sentiment. So, by the 1890's, concerts, plays, orations and other entertainments were staged by the various parishes once the parade ended. Prominent Irish dramatic and literary societies and the Ancient Order of Hibernians became an integral part of the celebrations for the next five decades. Although the Church to some degree controlled these entertainments and prohibited vaudeville acts from the programs, the concerts attracted an ecumenical audience of Irish nationalists, Catholics, Protestants and members of the Sant-Jean Baptiste Society.

Home Rule for Ireland was generally the underlying theme of the various programs. In 1890, life-sized portraits of "Ireland's Redeemer," British Prime Minister William Gladstone and "The Uncrowned King of Ireland," Charles Parnell, were carried through the streets. During Gladstone's years in office, he had unsuccessfully campaigned for a system of Home Rule for Ireland but was never able to get enabling legislation through the House of Lords. The morning of the 1890 parade was frosty as the Marshal-in-

Chief Charles McGuire tried to muster "a cold-looking procession." Because of the sharp winds, "for awhile it looked as if there was no system or organization." The *Star* noticed that "The bandsmen presented a sad spectacle trying to produce music from the combination of ice and brass." There was nevertheless a good deal of enthusiasm displayed not only by those who took part, but by the spectators. As the *Gazette* reported: "All was green, everywhere was green, and nowhere was there not green."

That evening, Queen's Hall was packed to the rafters for the St. Patrick's Night concert with everyone in the audience "wearing o'the green in buttonhole or bonnet." A music program was followed by a lantern show of "dissolving views of Ould Ireland," and the songs performed "received the hearty plaudits of the great audience." St. Ann's staged *Robert Emmett* and *Pat's Dilemma*, and at Victoria Hall there was a production of *Kathleen Mavourneen*, about a servant girl who returned to her humble beginnings after being disillusioned by her marriage to an aristocrat. The play was an original script by J. Rooney Martin, one of Montreal's earliest playwrights.

Elaborate decorations for the 1891 procession were "of a much better order than in the past." Five arches, some of a "political complexion" were erected along the route. The largest one on Wellington St. had two towers six metres high with a cross in the middle and on the face of the towers the outline of two elaborate harps 12 feet high. "It looked like a city in holiday attire," wrote one reporter, "a city gay, cheerful and animated." The day was somewhat cold, "but not too much to make the walk unpleasant in any way. The frosty weather had one decidedly favourable effect in hardening up the streets, making walking pleasant. Before the parade marshalled by Michael Shea was over, however, the streets had become slightly sloppy." At St. Patrick's, Haydn's First Grand Mass in B-flat Major, "Harmoniemesse" had its Montreal premiere. The Mass, however, was disrupted by "urchins" who handed out advertising flyers in the church for a waterfront tavern.

"Handkerchiefs were waved and many shouted and cheered until they were hoarse," as Sir John Sparrow Thompson, the first Roman Catholic prime minister and the first of Irish descent, took part in the 1892 celebrations. Thompson remarked on the fact that the parade had become "non-political and non-religious." It was a perfect day. Alderman Patrick Kennedy who had been elected to the legislature two weeks earlier, again marshalled the parade. This time he made a show of it. According to the *Herald*, he rode astride a horse "whose spirit was so warlike as to put the lives of her Majesty's subjects with some jeopardy." Kennedy himself, the *Herald* continued, was a "vision of dazzling splendor as to hurt the naked eye to look at it. That collar of gold about a yard broad and covered with golden shamrocks was a dream. Over this was a gold chain, a yard broad, and at the end of the chain there was a large cross studded with red and green brilliants and which coruscated in the sun with the baleful light like the gleam you see in the eye of one of Barnum's snakes. His hat was tall and shining like a mirror."

Father Dowd had died the previous December and there were "universal expressions of regret that [he] was no longer amongst the followers of the patron saint." With Dowd gone, however, "internal discord" surfaced among the representatives of the rival parishes and societies.

In 1893, several parishes formed a new organizing committee to run the parade, known as the Irish Catholic Association. It required a quota of men from each parish based on the size of the congregation to walk in the parade. Flagpoles were painted green and placed seven metres apart along the parade route to display the Canadian, Irish and papal flags. The St. Ann's Young Men's Society appeared in black suits and tall silk hats. Grand Marshal James Milloy, a founding member of the Catholic Sailor's Club, walked ahead of Montreal Hackmen's Union.

March 17, 1894, was a Palm Sunday. "There were no new features in the procession to speak of, but there was an abundance of enthusiasm both within and without the ranks," the *Gazette* reported. "The Irish jaunting car was there ... bands were numerous and the banners of the several societies and the splendid behaviour of those taking part." That year's parade marshal, Alderman Daniel Gallery, was a native of County Clare, Ireland. He had come to Canada as a youngster after his family had been evicted from their land at Slievedooley. Gallery accompanied the city's former Mayor, James "The People's Jimmy" McShane, who was trying to make a political comeback. A former minister of public works, he had been swept into office in 1891 as mayor but had lost in 1893. That evening, several plays including the *Shamrock and the Rose*, and *O'Rourke's Triumph of Irish Honour* were staged. Critics complained that the latter work written by a local playwright was "conspicuous by the absence of female roles."

The federal Liberal opposition leader Wilfrid Laurier had been expected to walk in the 1895 parade on Monday, March 18, 1895, but high winds buffeted the parade and he remained at home with the flu. The winds were so strong that many of the parade banners couldn't be unfurled. "There were more boys and bands than usual. Perhaps because the weather and the length of the walk prevented many of the older men taking part in it," suggested the *Gazette*. There were two large sleighs, one filled with girls labelled "Types of Erin's Daughters," the other crowded with boys, styled "Home Rulers." Mayor Joseph-Octave Villeneuve and his political rival, the former Mayor James McShane, president of the St. Patrick's Society, both wearing their chains of office, walked arm in arm to the delight of cheering bystanders.

In 1896, trains brought large numbers of visitors from Portland, Maine, bent on seeing the procession and the gaily decorated stores.

Queen Victoria celebrated her diamond jubilee in 1897, but the "great procession," that year marked the 50th anniversary of St. Patrick's Church which "never held a larger or more devout congregation." Among those in attendance was one Steven Corrigan who was present when the cornerstone for the church was blessed in September 1843. Under the direction of Marshal-in-Chief Alderman Tom Kinsella, the procession ventured for the first time below the hill along St. Patrick Street into the west end of the city as far as Charlevoix. "It was a great procession. There were great crowds, bright sunshine [...] The fates were propitious and seemed to have agreed that the best weather must be given for so auspicious an occasion. [...] The sun was a little strong and some of the more frequented roads were sloppy, but no one minded that. Three quarters of those who walked had in past years ploughed through several inches of mud. [...] The moneyed people [...] were in carriages. They were the envy of those who had to stand on the sidewalk."

It was cold and the streets a little muddy for the parade in 1898 but as the *Gazette* remarked, "Snow and ice have no power to daunt the Irish bent on celebrating Ireland's national saint." The lineup was typical, Marshal-in-Chief, Joseph O'Brien, walked in front of flags and a band, which was followed by a contingent from St. Gabriel's parish, with its own band and banners. Then came members of the Total Abstinence and Benefit Society. The congregation from St. Mary's with its own band and banners came next; members of the Holy Name Society with band and banners; then St. Ann's congregation. Papal cadets, "in their smart costumes and soldierly bearing" followed, with their own band and banners. Then came the congregation of St. Patrick's, boys from the Christian Brothers School, more bands and banners, members of the Young Irishmen's Literary Society, the Irish Catholic Benefit Society, St. Patrick's Total Abstinence Society, representatives from St. Bridget's, St. Patrick's band, and as was the custom, the mayor, William Prefontaine, and the clergy bringing up the rear.

On March 14, 1899, the Montreal Shamrocks cemented their Stanley Cup victory by winning a rematch against Queen's University. Three days later, a contingent of 1,500 members of the Ancient Order of Hibernians from Kingston, Ontario, swelled the ranks of the parade as they paid tribute to the winning team. The Hibernians arrived with about a hundred members of the Hibernian Knights, a para-military branch of their order—sporting high plumed hats, the knights under the command of Captain Patrick O'Kane. The knights first surfaced in 1892 at an AOH convention in St. Louis, Missouri, inspired in part by the Irish Volunteers who fought a rebellion against British rule in 1798. Publicly, the group was designed "to attract aggressively Catholic young men of good standing who wish to acquire a thorough knowledge of military discipline." Privately, it was a "secret" Irish patriotic fraternity, whose members were indoctrinated with the idea of "unifying Ireland as one nation." Spectators braved the cold winds as Parade Marshal Patrick J. O'Brien led the Hibernians, all of them "dressed in black and all [wearing] silk hats which gave them a striking appearance." The throngs were so large that the *Gazette* suggested many of those who lined the streets had to have come from east-end Montreal, "to admire the excellent showing. The West End, alone, could not have furnished the crowds which braved zero weather and biting March breezes to cheer on the shamrock-decked men must have been evident to anyone who saw the crowds which filled the sidewalks along the route."

Chapter Nine

By all accounts, the parade in 1900 was believed to be the first to attract residents from each and every one of the surrounding suburbs of the "Imperial city." Flags and bunting decorated most buildings, and shops were closed for the parade that Saturday morning. Queen Victoria had helped to spark the outpouring of Irish pride with the news that she was going to visit Ireland in April to drum up support for the Boer War. The Queen commanded her "loyal Irish troops" to wear the shamrock to support the "Irish boys in the Transvaal." Her appeal worked. Bystanders in Montreal turned out in record numbers in solidarity with the soldiers fighting the Boers and in a display of affection for the aging monarch who herself sported the shamrock. "It was almost impossible to find a man, woman or child in the streets who did not wear a sprig of shamrock or a green button of some kind," observed the *Gazette*'s reporter. In fact, demand that year was so great that a sprig of shamrock which normally sold for a nickel (worth about $2 today) sold for five times as much. Mayor Prefontaine (who was now also the Liberal member of Parliament for Maisonneuve) walked to St. Patrick's behind the Knights with Parade Marshal M.

McCarthy. The newly appointed apostolic delegate, Dio-
mande Angelo Falcanio Raymond celebrated the "Green'
Mass" at St. Patrick's. The dinner at the Windsor that evening
was described by one of the guests as "a beautiful tribute
to Shamrock Day." The guest speaker was Edward O'Brien
Kennedy, who had been jailed by the British for 16 years. His
remarks about the "unfaltering hatred of the British," did
not go down well with his Montreal audience which failed
to applaud. Home Rule for Ireland was the elephant in the
room, but Canadians for the most part wanted it achieved
through negotiation, not violence. The evening ended with
a slide show given by a visitor from Dublin which featured
stereoscopic views of "numerous nooks and places so dear
to the Irish heart."

Queen Victoria died in January 1901. Catholics were
prohibited from displaying any symbols of mourning for
a queen who once dismissed the Roman Catholic Mass as
little more than "superstitious idolatry." St. Patrick's Day that
year was on a Sunday, so the parade took place the following
Monday. An outbreak of scarlet fever thinned the ranks
of the participants, but Parade Marshal M. McCarthy and
Mayor Prefontaine were again prominent among those "big
men with tall hats, wreathed in shamrocks" who walked the
slushy streets.

There was no parade in 1902. Rev. John Quinlivan, who
had been pastor of St. Patrick's for ten years, died in Paris
on March 12 where he had gone to be treated for a medical
condition which had altered his personality. Organizers
explained that the procession had been cancelled because

Irish Catholics were in mourning for "a dead priest, dead in a strange land, far from the people with whom he dwelt in peace." Father Quinlivan had been responsible for the interior decoration of St. Patrick's where he was remembered as "one of those priests who was never too busy or too tired to hear the tales of those in trouble, all felt that he was their friend as well as their spiritual advisor." He was buried in Montparnasse. Members of the Ancient Order of Hibernians formed the guard of honour at the memorial Mass at St. Patrick's where Quinlivan's confessional box was draped in purple and gold.

In 1903, the Ancient Order of Hibernians dispatched a delegation from Ireland to Montreal to drum up support in Canada for Home Rule. They gained the sympathetic ear of Daniel Gallery, who by then was the influential Liberal Member of Parliament for St. Anne. There were two St. Patrick's parades that year, one in the east end organized by Rev. Patrick O'Callaghan, the pastor of St. Mary's whose church stood at the corner of St. Antoine and Panet. The other "official" march, organized with the assistance of members of the AOH, was a more militant undertaking led by Parade Marshal John F. Wheeler. According to the *Star* "Silk top hats which in former years had formed an almost inevitable accompaniment for the occasion were largely discarded. In their place was a soft hat with a band of white and green silk." The downtown parade was a subliminal appeal to Quebec nationalists to identify with Republican Irish sentiment. A distinctive Quebec flag with a white cross on a blue ground with white fleur-de-lis in each corner floated for the first time alongside the green Irish flag. It had been designed by Rev. Elphège Filiatrault to convey the not-too-subtle but symbolic message that French Canadians, like the Irish, "were a new nation, a new people on American soil, and a new people need a new flag." (The design of the flag was modified when it was officially adopted as Quebec's flag in 1948.)

The following year, 1904, "Erin's national colours were everywhere," the green flag bearing the golden harp flapped from hundreds of windows and households. The Irish not only gathered in numbers in 1904, and the parade, "large but not unwieldly" was according to *The Star* "a pronounced success." Behind the scenes however, relations between the parade's organizers and the quarrelling parish priests were strained.

Ten days before the 1905 parade there was a heated debate between the two factions over the parade route and on which day it should be held. The Ancient Order of Hibernians insisted it had to be held on the actual feast day; Members of the Irish Catholic Committee wanted it on the Sunday closest to the 17th. The Hibernians objected to "ragtime music," that the bands played as being "inappropriate," and insisted that only Irish airs were permissible. And it wanted to change the parade route and move it out of the Irish ghettos in order to "advertise their members, and influence and strengthen" the Irish presence in Montreal.

The rancour was so great, there was concern that the parade that year might be called off. "There has been a disposition on the part of some societies to withdraw from what has been a feature of the celebration for many years," the *Gazette* reported. But opposition was contained, and the parade was held on a warm spring day with Alderman Patrick J. Ryan as Marshal-in-Chief. It was a Friday, and the bishop allowed Catholics in the city to eat meat that year. "Nature […] lent her aid and Ireland's great day was a March gem," the *Gazette* reported. "Clear and bright overhead, the glorious spring sun beamed on earth, and the warm rays were beautiful evidence that old winter's hold [had] been broken. The spirit was in the air and it dominated people of various other nationalities. The gaiety of the Hibernians is infectious."

About 2,000 people and ten marching bands took part in the procession which went east to De Lorimier, then veered north to St. Catherine Street. and then headed west back along Dorchester for benediction at St. Patrick's Church. That evening, the St. Ann's Young Men's Society staged a play, *Galway Law*, about an Irish and a British lawyer who worked in the same law firm. The Young Irishmen's Literary and Benefit Society held a concert at Windsor Hall with "so many excellent features to the programme, but tersely, it may be said the entire affair was a pronounced success." Canada's Solicitor General, Rodolphe Lemieux, the Liberal MP for Gaspé and Solicitor General in Sir Wilfrid Laurier's cabinet delivered the most eloquent speech at that year's St. Patrick's dinner. "Ireland deserves Home Rule, not misrule," Lemieux told those powerbrokers in attendance, including Thomas Shaughnessy, Dr. William Hingston, and Judge Curran. "I see it coming, Irishmen are united today and Roman Catholics and Protestants alike join us in the demand. Home Rule is in sight. Home Rule will come."

From dawn to dusk, the whole day in 1906 was given up to the celebration, but the parade itself, marshalled by Alderman Thomas O'Connell, was smaller than usual.

In Ireland, the political Sinn Féin movement had been started "to promote in Ireland's capital a national legislature endowed with the moral authority of the Irish nation." Those who took part in Montreal's parade, according to one account, "seemed joyful though they had abundant opportunity of feeling otherwise by a moment's reflection on the traditions handed down in each Irish family, in exile or at home, that Ireland will one day be a nation."

St. Patrick's Day in 1907 fell on a Sunday, so the parade was held the following Monday. Filled with the sounds of "shrill pipe and resonant drum," it made its way east along Craig Street to Papineau, up Papineau to St. Catherine then west to Phillips Square, "Along every main thoroughfare in the city, long processions wended their way to St. Patrick's Church—sturdy-faced boys, young men in the prime of life, and grey haired veterans of many by-gone years." The Montreal chapter of the Ancient Order of Hibernians boycotted the parade and marched in Quebec City instead.

While the 1907 parade took place on "a delightful day blessed with glorious springtime," parade day the following year was so cold the shamrocks froze. Still, the turnout in 1908 was large. "The regalia had the freshness of spring and the inspiring music, both lively and melancholy, summed up what St. Patrick's Day has stood for in the hearts of Irishmen

The 1910 parade was one long line of marvel.
Montreal Star

for centuries." The decorations were not as elaborate as usual, but people taking part in the parade seemed to be younger and the teenaged participants seemed to be everywhere. "Some fifty or so mounted youngsters each wearing green blouses, short corduroy breeches with green stockings, and perhaps a cocked hat, gave a characteristic touch to the celebration." At the dinner the country's celebrated poet, William Henry Drummond, who had come to Canada from County Leitrim when he was ten years old, recited some verse he had written for the occasion, *We're Irish, Yet*, a poem which celebrates "the spirit of Celt":

> The breed that spurned the alien breast,
>   And every wrong has felt—
> And still, tho' far from fatherland,
>   We never can forget
> To tell ourselves, with heart and hand,
>   We're Irish yet! We're Irish yet!
> And they outside the clan of Conn
>   Would understand, but fail,
> The mystic music played upon
>   The heart-strings of the Gael—
> His ear, and his alone, can tell
>   The soul that lies within,
> The music which he knows so well,
>   The voice of Kith and Kin.
> He hears the tales of old, old days
>   Of battle fierce by ford and hill,
> Of ancient Senachie's martial lays,

And race unconquered still.
It challenges with mother's pride
*   And dares him to forget*
That, tho' he cross the ocean wide,
*   He's Irish yet! He's Irish yet!*
His eye may never see the blue
*   Of Ireland's April sky,*
His ear may never listen to
*   The song of lark on high,*
But deep within his Irish heart
*   Are cloisters, dark and dim,*
No human hand can wrench apart,
*   And the lark still sings for him.*
We've bowed beneath the chastening rod,
*   We've had our griefs and pains,*
But with them all, we still thank God,
*   The Blood is in our veins,*
The ancient blood that knows no fear,
*   The Stamp is on us set,*
And so, however foes may jeer,
*   We're Irish yet! We're Irish yet!*

There were two St. Patrick's parades again in 1909. Father Patrick O'Callaghan, the pastor of St. Mary's, once again held his own parish parade. The day would, however, be far more memorable in the city's history for another reason. At 9:30 that morning, just as Archbishop Bruchési began to celebrate the Mass at St. Patrick's, a train from Boston on its way to Montreal exploded as it arrived in Windsor Station

97

and sent a blast of scalding steam through the locomotive. An engineer and the fireman, both badly burned, leapt from the train which continued to pick up speed as it barrelled along the tracks and raced downhill to the terminal building. The runaway train crashed through the walls of the Ladies Waiting Room in Windsor Station before it roared to a halt in the main concourse of the building. Six people, including the train's conductor and three children were killed. Over the objections of some who wanted the parades cancelled because of the accident, both went ahead. Each followed different routes. In the east end, O'Callaghan's march wound its way up Papineau, along St. Catherine, to de Montigny, and De Lorimier and back along Dorchester to the church. The other parade went from St. Patrick's down Beaver Hall Hill through Victoria Square, along St. Antoine to St. Denis then along St. Catherine back to Phillips Square. It was a grey dull day with light snow which threatened to turn into a blizzard. But as the *Star's* reporter noted, Irishmen take little heed of the weather: "They have waded through slush, snow or have been buffeted by blizzards, yet enjoy every minute of the festivities." The St. Patrick's dinner went ahead that evening at the Windsor Hotel as planned. Federal Opposition leader Robert Borden; the minister of railways, George Graham; and Henri Bourassa, were the guest speakers. "With the electrified *"cille mill fate"* greeting the eye of all who entered the banquet hall, with ensigns of Erin displayed on every available space on the wall, and with every guest bedecked with a bit of green or a shamrock, the 53rd annual banquet was held."

Amateur groups staged a wide variety of entertainments throughout the city; you could take in the *Boys of Drogheda* at St. Mary's, *Grand Bugcall Erie* at the Monument National, *Savoureen Delish* at Stanley Hall, *Rosaleen* at the Princess Theatre or attend a lecture given by Matthew Cummings, the National President of the Ancient Order of Hibernians.

Chapter Ten

MONTREAL WAS PREPARING to host the World Eucharistic Conference in 1910, and the St. Patrick Parade that year was in some respects a dress rehearsal for the parades that would take place six months later as part of the first conference of Roman Catholic clergy to be held in North America. The 1910 St. Patrick parade stretched for six city blocks and the seemingly endless procession was described as "one long line of marvel."

Archbishop Bruchési was prompted to declare that the parade was a celebration of faith and religion. "I see the Irish Catholics of Montreal surrounded by Irish archbishops and by bishops from Ireland, England and the United States. Let us unite to make the coming Eucharistic Congress one worthy of the event. Unlike other nations on your feast day, you celebrate not a worldly victory nor a great battle, but you honour your birth in the faith of Christ."

Parade Marshal Alderman Thomas O'Connell and Mayor Guerin were at the head of the parade and attended the St. Patrick's dinner that evening, where Sir Thomas Shaughnessy, the U.S.-born president of Canadian Pacific Railways, delivered an impassioned speech in favour of Home Rule for Ireland.

"For generations there has been something in the nature of a feud between the people of Great Britain, or should I say, of the governing class of Great Britain, and the Irish. [...] I must declare my conviction that in the relations between Ireland and the other portions of the British Empire, there is a situation which should not and cannot longer continue. The direction of the world thought and world action has in recent years been toward reconciliation and compromise. The great employers of men have learned the lesson. They can no longer say 'my will and mine alone will prevail.'" He suggested that a legislative solution, along the lines of the British North America Act, which brought Canada into being, would "remove an ugly sore from the body politic of the Empire by according Ireland control of her internal affairs."

Saint Patrick's Night was also marked with presentations of *The Kerry Cow* and *Wicklow*. Edward VII died six weeks after the parade and his son, the Duke of Cornwall, became George V. The Liberal minority government in Westminster removed the power of the House of Lords to veto Home Rule for Ireland and Prime Minister Henry Asquith promised to introduce enabling legislation for the third time.

The prospect of Home Rule seemed brighter than ever as high-spirited participants in Montreal braved bitter winds in 1911, as representatives from nine English-speaking parishes, with the exception of St. Anthony's, took to the streets. "Shop windows were decorated with masses of shamrocks, green ribbon and tokens of the day, while from many housetops flew the green banner and the golden harp." St. Patrick's raised the green ensign outside the church, with the Union Jack in the upper left-hand corner of the flag. "Everything spoke of the dawn of a new day of hope for those who remain in the old land." Four plays were staged in the evening, *Grand Ire*, *The Pride of Kildare*, *Irish Exile* and *Home Rule for Ireland*.

Horses had always been part of the parade, but in 1912 as the *Star* reported, "Saddle horses were bedecked in surprisingly greater numbers with the green of the day, and ridden by marshals, sub marshals, presidents and officials of the many branches of Irish societies, to say nothing of the multifarious small boys on ponies of all conditions and ages."

About 3,000 took part in the proceedings that Monday, March 18, including one George Craven who, it was said, had marched in every parade since 1856. Although Patrick Lloyd was the Marshal-in-Chief, the festivities focused on the visiting bishop from Helena, Montana, John Patrick Carroll, an American who had studied for the priesthood in Montreal.

Carroll was in the city to raise money for the cathedral he was building in Montana and had preached a week-long retreat. On Sunday, he celebrated Mass. "The dignity and religious atmosphere of the service lifted the whole celebration far from the mere parade stage into the realms of the divine, forming a magnificent climax to the festival," remarked the *Gazette,* adding that the "near holiday aspect" of the occasion lasted in the streets long after the procession had ended.

Carroll attended the St. Patrick's Day concert at the Monument National. There he told the audience that Irish music united "the hearts and minds of the sea-divided Gael," and that through music freedom-loving peoples every-where were brought together in unison with Ireland. The following evening as Bishop Carroll was being feted at a banquet at the Windsor, a fire broke out in the hotel's cloak room resulting in a power failure. Guests finished the meal in candlelight.

Congregations from nine parishes in the city and 13 marching bands participated in the 1913 parade which began marshalling before dawn in Victoria Square. "Green bedecked jockey boys on horseback prancing all over," went from Victoria Square east along St. Antoine to Bleury, north to St. Catherine, west to Peel, then east again along Dorchester to the Congress Gate at the back of St. Patrick's Church. That evening, audiences could take in two plays especially written for St. Patrick's Night, *Home Rule for Ireland* at the Monument National, and *The Pride of Kildare* at the Theatre des Nouveautés.

The parade in 1913 went ahead on Palm Sunday, the day before St. Patrick's Day. Sundays are not considered part of Lenten observances, so the parade was held on the Sunday instead of on "the real 17th of Ireland." "Should the experiment prove to be successful, the custom may be established of holding the parade on Sundays hereafter," the *Gazette* reported. (The 17th, incidentally, is an arbitrary date. One tale has it that the Irish, who could never agree on anything, had some factions saying Patrick was in fact born on March 8th, another faction insisted it was March 9, so a clergyman with the wisdom of Solomon combined the two digits and declared that the saint was born on the 17th.)

Parade Marshal Alderman Patrick Monahan led the

parade in which nine parishes participated, each parish sending on average, about 300 marchers. The parade was followed by full houses at each of the three Irish-themed dramas staged that evening: *Carroll O'Donough* staged by the St. Anne's Young Men's Society at the Monument National, *My Geraldine*, staged by the Young Irishmen's Society at the Princess, and *Ivy Leaf,* staged by the Ancient Order of Hibernians' dramatic club.

Parade organizers continued to squabble over the details, but in 1914 at last agreed that the parade would be held each Sunday before March 17, instead of the day itself, because it "would be an enormous gain over the old custom and allow more people to take part." Consequently, the parade on Sunday, March 15, 1914, moved uptown "to advertise the influence and strength" of the Irish. It began in Dominion Square, and walked down St. Catherine to Guy, "in every respect the biggest in the history of the parade to date." It took an hour to pass any given point, "and many visitors who happened to be in the city expressed amazement that there should be so many Irish people in the *Canadian metropolis.*" To the surprise of many, Alderman Médéric Martin, who was running for mayor, marched in the parade to solicit votes. "With such large crowds, it was amazing that such perfect order should prevail," noted the *Gazette.* "The more so as the steeds of a number of the green-clad cavalry became restive amid the uproar."

Canada was at war when the 1915 parade took place. An estimated 6,000 turned out for the procession, "a decidedly imposing demonstration of the solidarity of the Irish people of Montreal," for Home Rule in Ireland.

By January 1916, an Irish Regiment to serve in the Canadian militia had been established in Montreal with a "shamrock on the cap and a harp on the collar" of their uniforms. In a demonstration of "unfailing loyalty to Britain at a time of crisis," the Rangers began recruiting, and began raising operational funds to outfit the regiment. The St. Patrick's Society and the Irish Protestant Benevolent Society joined forces for the first time in 60 years, and the Union Jack was carried in the cavalcade as a symbol of Montreal's loyalty to the Empire at war. It moved west to Mountain, north to St. Catherine, west to Guy, then up to Sherbrooke, and doubled back east to Union and then broke up at Phillips Square. All went well until the Irish Rangers unfurled their regimental colours in St. Patrick's Church only to learn that open rebellion against the British had broken out in Dublin. *Éirí Amach na Cásca,* or the Easter Rising, as it was called, was doomed even before it began. The British crushed the revolt and sent 15 of its leaders to the firing squad. With the rising of 1916, the Ancient Order of Hibernians challenged the St. Patrick's Society and formally objected to uniformed soldiers taking part in any parade.

As tensions in Ireland mounted, the Canadian government proposed a referendum on conscription. The "monster parade" in 1917 led by Médéric Martin who had successfully been elected mayor was in part, a demonstration against conscription by the Irish who felt no loyalty to Britain. It was followed by a mass meeting in suburban St. Louis where the assembly passed a resolution against enforced military service.

The 1917 parade marked the 70th anniversary of St. Patrick's Church where the main altar was "festooned with ferns sprinkled with green lights and illuminated shamrocks." A Pontifical High Mass was celebrated by Archbishop Bruchési, and the parade served as a "tag day" to collect funds for St. Patrick's Orphanage.

Still stung by the Easter Rising abroad and the conscription crisis at home, the Irish Catholic Committee wanted the 1918 parade called off in protest against "the extraordinary conditions." As well, the Ancient Order of Hibernians objected to "the presence of soldiers" in the parade. The conscription act had become law, and it has been argued that many in the Irish community feared that any young Irishman in the parade who appeared fit enough would be drafted into the military. The Ancient Order of Hibernians insisted that the 1918 parade be billed as an anti-war protest demonstration. The death of the Irish par-liamentary leader John Redmond on March 6, however, offered ICC organizers a convenient excuse to call off the parade that year. Cancelling the parade to mourn an Irish politician who was reviled in Ireland did not sit well with returning regiments. Redmond had thrown his support behind the British War effort in exchange for Home Rule. Many regiments of Irish descent seethed at the way they had been treated by the British, and that sentiment underscored the extent to which the diaspora and the homeland were now diverging. While Ireland itself was convulsed in 1918 with the reality of the looming Anglo-Irish war, the Montreal Irish were still paying homage to Redmond and consequently to a vision of Ireland as a place of the ancestral past.

Alderman William Hushion was grand marshal several times

Patrick McManamy rides in the 1922 parade.

Instead of a parade, a funeral Mass for Redmond was celebrated and as the *Herald* reported, "The procession of Irishmen and youths in colours and costumes perpetuating the traditions and incidents of the history of their ancestral land will be missing this year."

By the time the parade was revived in 1919, the Ancient Order of Hibernians again held sway in its organization. The *tridhathach nah Eireann*, the green, white and orange flag of the fledgling Republic of Ireland was carried through the streets, as participants defied the cold rain, strong winds, and slippery sidewalks that were lined with "kilted soldiers and doughboys." Marshal William James Hushion led the parade as he would each year for the next three until he was elected to the National Assembly.

As the *Star* pointed out, "The Ancient Order of Hibernians made a splendid show and looked well. St. Ann's Young Men's Society, which brought up the rear, also made a good impression." For the first time in 21 years, Archbishop Bruchési didn't celebrate Mass at St. Patrick's. The official story was that he was on a pilgrimage to Rome, to "the blessed spot where the heart of Daniel O'Connell was preserved." (O'Connell had been on a pilgrimage to Rome when he died in Genoa in 1847.) In fact, the archbishop had become delusional and had been admitted to hospital for psychiatric treatment.

In December, Sinn Fein won the general election in Ireland and Ireland declared its independence.

Chapter Eleven

In 1920, the Irish Catholic Committee turned the exclusive management of the parade over to The Ancient Order of Hibernians. The AOH says its records are "private files," so the reasons for the transfer are unclear. The AOH constitution, however, required the parade to be held on the actual saint's day, the 17th of March. The pastor of St. Patrick's, Gerald McShane, attempted to talk them out of that idea. Holding the parade on a Sunday, "in anticipation" of the date itself for the past seven years had, he argued, proven not only to be both popular with the public but profitable for the parish. "What is worth doing is worth doing well, and we cannot remain indifferent to the holding of this traditional demonstration," McShane wrote in the church bulletin, *The Messenger*. "We make an appeal to all our men to turn out strong on the afternoon of the 14th." So, on Sunday, March 14, 1920, Bishop Georges Gauthier celebrated the "Mass of Anticipation," at St. Patrick's. There was snow underfoot "and heaps of it," with a bright sun overhead. After the parade, a four-act play, *Kitty O'Hara*, was staged. But the rift between the AOH and McShane had not been settled. The Ancient Order of Hibernians unilaterally decreed that the parade the following year would be held on March 17th, a Thursday. In response, McShane said he would no longer celebrate a Green Mass in St. Patrick's unless the parade was staged on a Sunday. "It does not appear as if many will participate this year in the parade on St. Patrick's Day," declared an article in the *St. Patrick Messenger*. "It is more than evident that the people as a whole would not be sorry to see the parade discontinued. For the past 13 years, the pastor, in the pulpit and by the printed word, has appealed to his parishioners to maintain the ancient usage, advising the men to take an interest in the celebration and turn out in large numbers with their parish priest. The net result after all this pleading and pressure was that not ten per cent of the men would put in an appearance, and St. Patrick's always paraded with a slender line up."

As a result, the Ancient Order of Hibernians arranged to have the Mass in 1921 celebrated at St. Ann's. "So great were the crowds that extra seating had to be furnished, and people who could not get inside stood outside the church before the parade began," observed the *Gazette*. For the next few years, the official Mass would alternate on the saint's day among other churches: St. Ann's, St. Gabriel's, St. Mary's, and St. Thomas Aquinas. Alderman William James Hushion marshaled 900 members of the Ancient Order of Hibernians and members of their women's auxiliary, "who looked well and marched well," in the 1921 parade. A squad of mounted city police officers followed and there was "a good turnout of schoolboys, who trudged along with as much determination as their elders." Among them was 12- year-old Frank Hanley, who always claimed he was expelled from school for walking without permission in the parade that year. Hanley would grow up to be a ward boss in Pointe Ste. Charles and one of the city's most colourful characters. That evening, *The Dear Irish Boy* was staged at Theatre St. Denis, and *Arrah Na Pogue* at the Monument National.

Pope Pius XI was crowned in February, 1922, Ireland was partitioned in May and the Irish Free State was proclaimed in December. The events were celebrated with a new spirit of enthusiasm that infused the parade held on Saint Patrick's Day in 1922. A portrait of the Protestant Irish Nationalist Charles Stewart Parnell who had led the fight for Home Rule was carried through the streets inscribed with the words "*Let No Man set Bounds to the onward March of a Nation.*" St. Patrick's Church observed its 75th anniversary on March 17, 1922, but did not participate in that year's parade. McShane ruled that "because the season of lent and winter would be most unsuited for the elaborate program we have in view for our diamond jubilee, and most inconvenient for the number of visitors and guests we expect," the milestone would be marked with three days of celebrations in mid-October.

In 1923, Parade Marshal Captain Toby Kavanaugh led 18 units to St. Gabriel's Church for the unveiling of a painting, *Saint-Patrick en route pour Tara* by Georges Delfosse, a Quebec artist who produced hundreds of works for churches in the province. (It was lost in the fire that gutted the church in 1956.) Seven thousand turned out for the parade, the first since Ireland won its independence, but many in the crowd wore black arm bands to mourn the death of Michael Collins who had been murdered by the IRA the previous August. Kavanaugh was greeted at the door of St. Gabriel's by the parish priest, James McCory. "St. Gabriel's was decorated in Irish colours for the occasion without and within. Inside, special green lights were on, and about the altar illuminated harps and shamrocks." A priest from Notre Dame, Indiana, James French, preached a homily on the subject of "reverence for women." When the service ended the parade continued, with young jockeys on horseback, dressed in green, who cantered up and down the parade route. Four months later, in July, 10,000 members of the Ancient Order of Hibernians arrived in Montreal for an International Convention held at the Windsor Hotel. Mayor Médéric Martin welcomed delegates, telling them "It is the right of different nations to fight for their countries, and the day is not far off when you will have your liberty in Ireland."

More than a thousand volunteers canvassed the streets during the 1924 parade and raised more than a quarter of a million dollars for the St. Patrick's Orphanage. Horses weren't allowed in parade that year, but the Hibernian Knights with their green feathered helmets led delegations from 11 parishes and 18 marching bands. They wound their way along Dorchester, down Beaver Hall Hill then along St. James to St. Ann's for Mass. "While the snowy background and chill air made the day bleaker than usual, the walking was better than for many a celebration," the *Star* noted. Mayor Médéric Martin, in a fight for his political life, was in the parade, as was Victor Morin, the head of the Saint-Jean Baptiste Society and Edward Earl, from the Protestant Benevolent Society. (Martin would lose the mayoralty election three weeks later to Charles Duquette.) Toby Kavanaugh was again the grand marshal.

The following year, 1925, Alderman Frank Hogan, president of the Montreal Athletic Commission (and later president of the National Boxing Association), was parade marshal. "The weatherman, as usual, showed he was a poor Irishman and turned on a depressing drizzle. But rain or no rain, the loyal descendants of Ireland refused to be dampened and arrayed in all varieties of the national colour." They paraded the streets to St. Aquinas Church where Mass was celebrated.

Children from the Christian Brothers, St. Ann's School, members of the St. Patrick's Labour Club and the Irish Immigrant Society swelled the ranks of the parade on March 17, 1926. "The shamrock was seen everywhere, not alone in the procession but in the caps of laborers along the route, in the lapels of businessmen and close to the hearts of colleens and their mothers and brothers and sisters," observed the *Gazette*. Frank Hogan marshalled the parade which made its way to Saint Gabriel's for mass that year.

The sun was shining, there was no snow, and grass in Montreal's parks was green on March 17, 1927, for one of the warmest parade days on record. There were no representatives from Sinn Féin that year as Joseph Dillon, the Liberal MLA for St. Anne's, was parade marshal. It was also the first year that the parade blocked traffic, "and tramways and vehicles of all kinds were tied up for blocks around Victoria Square as the procession made its way to the church of St. Thomas Aquinas."

John Loye rides a sidecar in the 1927 parade.

A carnival atmosphere infused the parade on Thursday, March 17, 1928, which was a little less reverential and more festive than it had ever been. Elaborate and expensive allegorical floats depicting religious and patriotic events in Irish history—*The conversion of the Druids, St. Patrick at Tara,* and *the Rock at Cashel*—rolled along St. Catherine to St. Ann's Church "under sunny skies and warm spring weather." The imaginative floats that beefed up the parade were designed by John Loye, an amazingly energetic but private 46-year-old graphic artist and amateur historian who was inspired by the jubilant atmosphere of the annual St. Jean Baptiste Parade. (He also designed the Irish societies chain of office which links 12 shamrocks together with the arms of the four provinces of Ireland: Leinster, Munster, Connacht, and Ulster.) A tall, earnest man with an aquiline face, Loye was a confirmed bachelor with an artistic bent. He had been born in Montreal in 1880 and raised as a militant Irish republican who had nothing but disdain for anything British. Later as President of the United Irish Societies, the organization which he helped to start, he would be the one-man band who kept the parade running through 26 difficult years.

The 1928 parade under "sunny skies and spring weather" saw several new features. A contingent of the Montreal police force was at the head of the march and floats representing the various parishes on the island "who couldn't be represented in line," made their way from Dominion Square to St. Patrick's where a priest from St. Vincent's Priory in New York preached the sermon, then it continued to St. Thomas Aquinas where the Green Mass was celebrated by Archbishop Gauthier.

The positive public reaction to the 1927 and 1928 parades inspired Loye to build on its success. He suggested that the English-speaking Roman Catholic parishes on the island unite to create what he initially called the United Irish League of Montreal. "Our present St. Patrick's Day demonstration, good as it is, is not as good as it should be," he wrote in a proposal circulated to the various parish priests, in which he recommended that they unite in "spirit and good will and resolution," to form the United Irish Societies. Its objective, Loye suggested to its founding executives, John McCaffrey and William Hickey, would be to "increase our marching strength," and "reclaim to some small degree those of our race who are willing to lead back to the timely custom on marking St. Patrick's Day by an imposing demonstration (which might become) one of the outstanding events of the American continent."

Loye's inspiration had always been "the worthy example of the French Canadians who spare no expense in making the celebrations of Saint-Jean Baptiste Day one to attract the interest in the comment of the whole continent." The proposed societies' mission statement, he wrote, would be "to unite and solidify Irish Catholic sentiment towards Irish out-of-door demonstrations in Montreal and the vicinity. …we are well aware there are many of our people in the far-flung sections of our community who need but the invitation and direction from the proper course and they will join with us in maintaining the traditions of our community."

Under his persuasive new leadership, the 1929 parade was "organized and carried out without a hitch," by the

United Irish Societies which inaugurated a "St. Patrick's Week" of festivities which ended for the first time in a decade with Mass at St. Patrick's. Everyone agreed that the 17 allegorical floats Loye designed had invigorated that year's parade and equalled the quality of the floats in the annual June 24 Saint-Jean Baptiste Parade. This time, delegations from every Irish parish in Montreal led by Marshal-in-Chief Alderman Thomas Fagan took part in what was called "one of the largest and most picturesque turnouts."

Little did those who walked in that year's parade know that eight months later the world was headed into the Great Depression with the collapse of the stock market when everything went horribly wrong. With the financial panic and misery that followed, the survival of the parade was once again seriously threatened.

Chapter Twelve

"Affable, smiling and doffing his 'topper'; from left to right," Mayor Camillien Houde, who described himself as "the biggest French-Canadian leprechaun," walked the route to St. Patrick's in the two-hour parade on March 17, 1930. "Such a long procession, such wonderful floats, and such beautiful horses. So much to look at and everything went smoothly." Verdun was represented by its mayor, Charles Allen, riding in an open limousine behind the float that Verdun had entered depicting "The Minstrel Boy." It was one of a number of allegorical floats in the parade sponsored by the various parishes that year including, "The Old Weir Bridge at Killarney' (St. Patrick's parish) "The Shamrock" (St. Willibrord's) "Ross Castle, Killarney" (St. Thomas Aquinas) "Abbey Ruins" (St. Michael's) "Celtic Cross " (Holy Cross parish) "St. Kevin" (St. Gabriel's) "St, Brendan" (St. Brendan) "St. Patrick Driving the Snakes out of Ireland" and "Blarney Castle (St. Aloysius) and "The Bard of Erin," (St. Anthony's). The Ancient Order of Hibernians entered a float depicting Mount Cashel, the *Montreal Beacon* newspaper, a float called "The Last Glimpse of Ireland," and the St. Patrick's Society had a float depicting St. Patrick. A delegation from St. Raphael's, a recently created English-speaking parish, walked in the parade soliciting funds for the church it planned to build in Outremont. A squad of motorcycle police held back the crowds on the sidewalk. "Everything moved as if by clockwork and undoubtedly the parade was a success by every point of view."

By 1931, the economy was faltering, and unemployment surged as the Dow Jones stock market index slipped to its lowest level in history, bottoming out at 41.22. A federation of Catholic charities had been started to deal with the effects of the Depression in Montreal. In spite of increasing economic uncertainty, a cardboard model of the proposed St. Mary's Hospital was one of the floats in the mile-long parade on Sunday, March 15, 1931. "A colourful parade it was, but mostly one colour, green" is how the *Gazette* described it. "Bands played *The Wearing of the Green*, sprigs of shamrocks adorned hats, and buttonholes and the golden harp on green made a flaunting display." Patriotism for "John Bull's Other Ireland," was also manifest.

Mayor Houde again walked with Grand Marshal Alderman Kavanaugh ahead of the municipal police force which strode along four abreast, wearing "shamrocks and revolvers," and the Irish constables with their "green and white plumes." The most memorable float, many agreed was the one which depicted women from St. Willibrord's parish making lace and linen. That evening The Ancient Order of Hibernians staged *Hearts Desire,* at His Majesty's Theatre. The program notes that one Frank Hanley, then 21 years old and already on his way to making a name for himself, was in the cast of the romantic comedy of errors.

Mayor Camillien Houde, described himself as "the biggest French-Canadian leprechaun."

1932 marked the 1,500th anniversary of St. Patrick's arrival in Ireland. In Montreal a "solid phalanx" of Irishmen braved chilly winds on March 13 to enact the theme of the parade, "Our Heritage." (March 20 that year was Palm Sunday.) A Movie Tone camera filmed the event for newsreels in the cinemas. District fire chief Patrick "Paddy" Doolan, who had been twice decorated for bravery, led a contingent of 20 Irish police constables along Dorchester to St. Mathieu, back east along Sherbrooke and down Union to St. Patrick's. (Doolan would be arrested four years later, in July 1936, and charged with the beating deaths of his wife and 20-year-old son but was later declared mentally unfit to stand trial.) The *Star* reported:"Sure, this was a St. Patrick's Day and all, shiny toppers grit with shamrocks came along to prove it. Stalwart Irishmen strode under top hats and from the rear floated the sentimental melody, *I'll Take you back again Kathleen.*"

The election of John Loye as President of the United Irish Societies in 1933 injected a measure of stability during the darkest days of the Depression. Loye was committed to keeping the parade alive. "There is no dampening of spirits of the Irish parishes, on the contrary, they are determined to banish from the land the shade of depression as the saint himself banished the snakes from Ireland," Loye declared upon taking up the chain of office. There were, however, no floats in the parade marshaled that year by Inspector "Paddy" Lawton on Sunday, March 19. Snow had melted, leaving puddles in the streets. It was a case of what was described as "water, water all the way, but not a float in sight." Parishes could no longer afford to build them. "Smitten by all embracing need for economy, […] the

Irish displayed their numerical strength without the allegorical cars of yester-year. But there were by actual count, 454 top hats, including fifteen on horseback, nine in automobiles. Shamrock sprigs worn either in hat or buttonhole or both, numbered 19,260 sprigs of shamrock according to a group of Irish lads who stood in front of the Architects' building and counted them. Green-ribboned canes numbered about 10,000. Bog-oak shillelaghs and slim blackthorn cudgels [...] were so conspicuous by their absence that the reporter did not see one," the *Gazette* assured its readers.

Four rockets were fired to signal the start of the parade: the first at 3 o'clock warned the marchers to take their places, the second was a signal to get ready, the third to go, and the fourth was fired to announce the presence in the parade of Mayor Rinfret and the various dignitaries. The *Star's* account paid attention to the "gleaming toppers wreathed in shamrocks, green clad riders curbing horses that were frightened by the blare of bands and thousands upon thousands of marchers proudly ribboned with emerald." The annual dinner that year was a modest "stag" affair for 200 men.

1934 also marked the centennial of the St. Patrick's Society. Prime Minister Richard Bedford Bennett, Lord Shaughnessy, E.W. Beatty, the president of the CPR, and Nova Scotia's Premier Angus Macdonald were all present at the dinner in the Windsor Hotel for the event. The chief of Montreal's fire department, Christopher Carson, said to be the first Protestant to be named Grand Marshal, swapped the idea of riding on horseback in parade for the comfort of a ride in an open convertible. "They came down Sherbrooke Street thousands strong, prancing horses, plumed knights and decorated automobiles, with bands blaring and flags flying under a canopy of tree branches that had turned to silver icicles in the grey cold of the afternoon. White snow and the dull light made the shamrocks look greener as they dangled from hat bands and button holes," suggested the *Gazette* reporter. "Silk hats came in a mass, tilted left and tilted right, or stuck solidly in the middle of a good Irish head."

1934 not only marked the 50th anniversary of St. Ann's parish but was also the centennial of the Saint-Jean Baptiste Society. Loye wanted to do "something big" to celebrate the shared anniversaries. He proposed that the Irish and the French combine forces to stage one big bash on June 24. Loye pitched the idea to his old friend Dr. Victor Morin, a past president of the SJBS. He proposed sending a company of uniformed Hibernian Knights which formed "a living cross," led by a brass band to the June celebrations. It appeared it might happen. Loye began looking for sponsors. But he had overstepped his authority both with the St. Patrick's Society and with the Société.

On June 13, ten days before the SJB parade, the Saint-Jean Baptiste Society's Conseil générale rejected the idea because Loye had not invited any of its members to take part in the St. Patrick's Parade the previous March. The concept, it said, was "inconsistent avec le sentiment certain que la société a été la planification." Loye later admitted that he had taken his friendship with Morin for granted and that he should have gone through the proper channels to seek the opinion of the executive of the Society.

"Leaden skies and fitful showers of sleet and rain driven by strong winds" had no effect on those who marched in the 1935 parade on Sunday, March 17. "Banners and flags whipped in the strong winds, citizens in many instances set flags on their houses and the Number 10 Police Station was a blaze of colours with shields of flags on its facade and a huge Union Jack hung across the street side by side as the fire chief, took the salute as chief reviewing officer. But the loudest cheers were reserved for Mayor Camillien Houde who had been returned to office in the 1934 election. "Irishmen remain free to the tradition of Erin and at the same time are Patriots of Canada," read an editorial in the Gazette. "Sober thousands marched and thousands of others lined the route, all races and religions being represented. The presence of so many boys and youths in the ranks gave promise that the memory of St. Patrick will be kept green in this neighbourhood for years to come."

The parade in 1936 was especially noteworthy because for the first time, a woman rode in an open convertible with her husband, Verdun alderman Thaddeus Kilfeathe, at a time when women were not permitted to be in the parade. It would be another seven decades before another woman, Mabel Fitzgerald, would be named chief reviewing officer. The parade celebrated the centennial of the founding of the Ancient Order of Hibernians and delegations from Quebec City, Sherbrooke, Ottawa, and Toronto swelled its ranks on parade day, March 15. There were chants of "*On the 17th of March watch them coming down the line, on the 17th of March everyone looks fine,*" as they made their way through the streets.

The 1937 parade paid homage to the Irish *patriotes* who took part in the 1837 rebellion. The parade marshal mounted on horseback wasn't an Irishman, but a French-Canadian alderman, David Rochon whose mother was Irish. The weather was unseasonably mild on Sunday March 14 as close to 100,000 witnessed the march. "The air was just fresh enough to keep the marchers from lagging and soft enough for the comfort of the thousands of spectators who crowded the streets." A score of bands "purring music into the sky" played a tumult of Irish melodies. "If all the shamrocks that were twined around hats, stuck in buttonholes, pinned on breasts, draped on automobiles and hung around horses' necks, if all the shamrocks came from Ireland, the Ould Sod must be sadly denuded."

A steady downpour of driving rain on Sunday, March 20, 1938, threatened the cancellation of the parade, but John Loye was not about to call it off. Hundreds of spectators seeking shelter in doorways along Sherbrooke St. watched as a Sûreté du Québec squadron led the marchers through the rain and slush. Grand Marshal John Powell, national vice president of the Ancient Order of Hibernians, and Mayor Adhémar Raynault were drenched by the time the procession arrived at St. Patrick's.

The world was holding its collective breath in the spring of 1939 as it waited for the war that was inevitable. Adolph Hitler was in the final preparations for the Holocaust the Third Reich was about to unleash when more than 20,000 marched "hand in hand with the church" on March 19. They walked to St. Patrick's to pray for peace and to salute the election of Giovanni Pacelli as Pope Pius XII two weeks earlier.

Bright sunny weather brought crowds out in numbers larger than expected as Parade Marshal Dr. L. P. Nelligan, wearing a top hat bedecked with a green ribbon led the "proud Irishmen, three score and ten," and teenaged youngsters who added colour to the parade. There were, as the *Star* reported, "hundreds of traditional top hats, hundreds of traditional black thorn walking sticks, and scores of flags showing the golden harp of Ireland on a green field in the columns of the parade." But that sign of fealty to Ireland would have repercussions in Montreal in the days that lay ahead.

Chapter Thirteen

THE OUTBREAK OF HOSTILITIES in Europe in September 1939 threatened to sidetrack Montreal's St. Patrick's Parade for the duration of the Second World War. The problem was the declaration of Irish neutrality by Taoiseach Émon de Valera. By extension, the Irish in some quarters of Montreal were, like Italians, and later the Japanese, regarded with a measure of suspicion as being unpatriotic and branded as a threat to national security.

St. Patrick's Day in March 1940 fell for the first time since 1799 on a Palm Sunday and one week before a federal election which was being fought on whether or not to conscript Canadians. A number of local parish priests wanted to cancel the parade because they feared such a demonstration of Irish pride could be interpreted as support for Ireland's declared neutrality and seen as "a manifest of disloyalty" or even worse, as "an affront to the British Crown."

An early afternoon snowstorm threatened to make the day miserable, but the dark clouds gave way to sunshine and 10,000 men with palms and shamrocks arranged as a cross on their lapels (including a number of candidates running for political office), led by the pipes and drums of the Black Watch walked to St. Patrick's Church. Alderman Richard Quinn was the Marshal-in-Chief and walked with former parade marshal William Hushion, who had just been appointed to the Senate, and with Mayor Houde and Verdun's Mayor Edward Wilson. The Liberals won the March 26 election with just over 51 per cent of the vote. In August, Mayor Houde was arrested under the War Measures Act for suggesting men defy the call to register for military service and he was interned for four years. With so many enlisted men overseas and the majority of parish priests reluctant to take part, the 1941 effort was much smaller than usual. Women, who were not permitted to walk the parade, formed a large part of the bystanders who lined the sidewalks to watch as Marshal-in-Chief, Francis Connors, a pharmacist and the Liberal MNA for St. Anne's, and Senator Hushion waved to the crowds. Mayor Adhémar Raynault brought up the rear. Eighty-nine-year-old James McKenna, who claimed he had never missed a parade since 1860 took part for his 80th time. The biggest challenge during the war was staging the parade at all. By February 1942, 16 of the 22 English-speaking parish priests voted to cancel the parade.

John Loye wouldn't hear of it.

The parade, he insisted, was necessary to boost morale. "We were reproached by some for deciding to continue the parade. The reasons given were not very definite, but I have a definite opinion: only when a community is under the shadow of defeat and believes that its cause is lost, when it becomes hopeless and falls into despair, it forgets to celebrate. Until such a day comes, I will not abandon the parade. It is due to sustain and survive for many years to come. There has now developed a movement for its abolition."

Loye described the opposition as a "turning point in the long-established course of our annual celebration." He countered with a six-point argument of his own as to why the parade should continue.

1. It is a manifest of our presence as an influential section of the city's population.
2. It is a medium of introducing to public knowledge the leaders of our community.
3. It is purposely calculated to unify the English-speaking Catholic community.
4. It is a venerable institution of the City of Montreal and has been accepted by its citizens for over a hundred years.
5. It is now more firmly established in the order of our public events than it was in the past because it enjoys the cordial support and co-operation of the federal, provincial, and civic powers.
6. Because we should endeavour to preserve our identity as a community and not allow ourselves to dissolve and disappear into the common bulk of the population.

To compensate for the absence of "those parishes which have deserted our parade," Loye invited the police, the firefighters, and the Quebec Provincial Police to swell the ranks of those who marched. The 1942 parade during the darkest days of the war coincided with the 300th anniversary of Montreal's founding. As a patriotic tribute to Canada's fighting forces, contingents from the Army, Navy, and Air Force all took part. Pat Lynch was the grand marshal. Bishop Lawrence Whelan, who had been consecrated a bishop six months earlier, was also present. The Ukrainian flag, in support of the Ukrainian Insurgent Army, was carried in the parade even though it wasn't supposed to be. The only other complication that year arose when Loye refused to allow the toast to the King to be reinstated at the annual St. Patrick's banquet. He recommended that the playing of *God Save The King* be dispensed with. Loye, however, was over-ruled, and he resigned as chairman of the banquet committee. (But not as parade organizer.)

"The parade and banquet were discussed in all their aspects, and the matter of the toast to the King was considered. It was agreed that the presence at the dinner of Bishop Whelan made it obligatory to toast the reigning sovereign. This of course made it necessary for the chairman of the banquet committee to resign on principle," he explained.

There were calls to have Loye removed from his office completely for his "disloyalty." But not only did he survive a vote of confidence, he enlisted support from French-Canadian organizations. "With each recurring feast, we the organizers of the annual public celebrations find it more and more difficult to obtain material support from the English-speaking Catholic parishes," he complained. "In recent years we have encountered actual combined opposition from a certain number of parish priests. On the other hand, we have found a growing tendency to support and participate

IRELAND
NATION ONCE AGAIN

John Loye (standing) refused to allow the toast to the King
to be re-instated at the annual St. Patrick's banquet.

on the part of the French Canadians. They find it in their
interest to support us, one seems to justify the other, and
without one, the other might find itself uncomfortably
alone." Loye established "a new order and a new policy to
meet the changing attitudes of our community and to move
accordingly with the times."

He opened the society to women. "Fortune followed us
in '43," he boasted in his annual report. "We have had larger
parades in the past, but the demonstration in 1943 had
certain aspects which made it different." That it took place at
all was reason enough for Loye to be satisfied. "For reasons
well understood, many were afraid the street parade would
not be held this year. When it was decided to proceed, many
regarded the venture as ill-timed and ill-advised."

To counter claims that the parade was unpatriotic, Loye had invited generals and admirals to take part. A platoon of 60 provincial police and traffic officers, followed by firefighters, led the 1943 parade on March 21 which was held to mark the centennial of the laying of the cornerstone of St. Patrick's Church. Thomas Patrick Healy, the Member of Parliament for St. Ann's and a city councillor, was the grand marshal. One of the "brightest and most Irish," of the colour units was St. Willibrord's high school cadet band. Mayor Adhémar Raynault who was with the official civic party declared that the parade was "just like the Saint-Jean Baptiste!"

The parade in 1944 "still finds us under the canopy of war," Loye observed. "Many of those who filled our ranks in our annual parade have gone overseas, and some as you know will never return." Army, navy, and air force units again took part in that year's parade which braved "wild March winds and fair weather," on March 19. The parade featured a motorcade with cars displaying banners with the number of enlisted men from each of the respective parishes who were serving overseas. Parade Marshal alderman Thomas Guerin turned up wearing his lieutenant colonel uniform. "It was a great day for the Irish, and they showed it by displaying more green than is evident in the entire Emerald Isle," noted the *Gazette*.

Frank Hanley, always a lively presence in any parade, was named Grand Marshal in 1945. Brazen and bumptious, "Banjo" Frank Hanley, as he was called, had been a popular featherweight boxing champion in Pointe St. Charles and a jockey before he started the St. Ann's Community Council.

Frank Hanley was named grand marshal in 1945.

As a 30-year-old bantam of a man with roots in the neighbourhood, he was elected to council as an independent in 1940. He quickly rose through the ranks to become a member of the city's Executive Committee and acting mayor for the four years that Mayor Camillien Houde was incarcerated for sedition.

After Houde returned and was re-elected mayor with an overwhelming majority, he was greeted with roars of approval as he once again took part in the parade. It was an unusually warm sunny Sunday afternoon, and the streets were crowded with the Irish and those who wished they were. The war was coming to an end and the Legion carried flags of all nations in the two-hour parade as Major General

Léo Richer Laflèche, Minister of National War Services, took the salute on the reviewing stand.

"Walking along Sherbrooke one could see numerous followers of St. Patrick's: The tiny tot who wore a green ribbon in her hair but could speak only French, the U.S. Air Force lad from Alabama who drawled, 'we have millions and millions and millions of people in our St. Patrick's parade… […] Everything from *The Wearing of the Green* to *Jingle Bells* was played by the various bands in the parade.'"

A large military presence of uniformed Army, Navy and Air Force veterans were present in the first parade after the war in 1946. Grand Marshal Patrick Quinn, a Verdun city councillor, bumped along in the jaunting cart from the corner of Dorchester and St. Mathieu, down Sherbrooke to Union. That year his daughter, Helen, was the first woman to be admitted as a member of the United Irish Societies. It marked the beginning of the Quinn family's long and distinguished association with the parade which continues to the present day. St. Patrick's Day was a Sunday that year and Bishop Charbonneau, resplendent in his *cappa magna* (a purple and gold vestment with a long train), celebrated Mass at St. Patrick's.

The parade in 1947 coincided with the centennial of St. Patrick's Church. Mayor Houde again walked "under skies as blue and sunny as those that sparkle on the shores of the Killarney Lakes," with Frank Hanley at his side. District court judge Thomas Coonan, a veteran of the First World War who had been a minister without portfolio in Maurice Duplessis' cabinet, was parade marshal.

A Mass of Anticipation was celebrated for the first time

the Sunday before the 1948 parade at St. Michael's and St. Anthony's Church in Mile End by Rev. Capt. Michael T. J. O'Brien, who was the grand marshal of that year's parade. Capt. O'Brien had been a chaplain with the Canadian Siberian Expeditionary Force sent to Vladivostok during the Russian Revolution in an attempt to persuade Russia to continue fighting in the First World War. He devoted much of his ministry to working with veterans of both World Wars. Just as that year's parade was about to begin, a torrential downpour hit the city and because of the storm the parade was officially cancelled. However, a large number of military units that had been through much worse were already lined up and waiting to start. They ignored the directive and began walking through the driving rain in what was later described as "an outlaw parade." As an RCAF Dakota Transport roared overhead, the rain stopped. Spectators returned to the streets and the parade was on. Father O'Brien, who thought the parade had been cancelled and was on his way home, was hastily rounded up and driven to the reviewing stand in front of Strathcona Hall on Sherbrooke St. Afterwards, Loye was chastised for his decision to call off the parade. In his report, he pointed out that he was damned if he did, and damned if he didn't. "Only twice in our 20 years of control of the parade have we been confronted with a wet day. On the first occasion (in 1938), I gave the word to carry on. I was reproved and criticized," he explained. "On the second occasion, I gave word to cancel." Loye admitted he could have called in the police to stop those units that decided to march anyway but didn't because he said he wanted "to save the dignity of the United Irish Societies."

The fact that the parade went ahead in spite of being officially cancelled that year gave rise to the widespread boast in the years afterwards that Montreal's parade had gone on without interruption since it began, "the longest continuous running St. Patrick Parade in the world." It would take another 70 years to put an end to that myth.

In 1949, three squadrons of the Royal Canadian Air Force staged a fly past as an estimated 75,000 lined the route. Fourteen parishes, 13 air cadet squadrons, the RCMP, two military units took part. General Ralph Otter Morton, who had been in command of the 1st Canadian Army troops during World War II, and now head of the Quebec command, was chief reviewing officer. Emmett McManamy, a prominent municipal court judge, of whom it was said "tempered justice with common sense if not exactly with mercy," was grand marshal.

The Quinn family were part of the parade for decades.

Chapter Fourteen

"THE IRISH LOOKING FOR THE best St. Patrick's Parade should come to Montreal instead of New York," declared city coun-cillor Edward O'Flaherty, the chief reviewing Officer fol-lowing the parade in 1950. It took place under sunny skies but with a March wind blowing. While the parade in New York was started by Irish soldiers in the British Colonial army in 1769 and is considered to be the oldest in North America in terms of demographics, O'Flaherty was right. Montreal, then with a population of 1.3 million, had a high-er percentage of participants than New York with 8 million did. Four Australian bishops were present at St. Patrick's for the Pontifical High Mass celebrated by Bishop Lawrence Whelan: Justin Simonds of Melbourne, Matthew Beovich of Adelaide, James O'Collins of Ballarat and Alfred Gummer of Geraldton. Mayor Houde again took the salute in the reviewing stand.

The United Irish Societies encountered "unprecedented difficulties," selecting a Grand Marshal for the 1951 parade. The position was initially again offered to Senator Hushion, who had previously marshalled the parade in the 1920s. Hushion fell ill. His son was set to replace him but, he too, cancelled one week before the event. That left organizers scrambling. Rev. John Gordon Carroll, a pastor at Holy Family parish was approached and accepted, but Carroll was forced to bow out by his bishop who ruled that "a public parade was no place for a priest." Finally, with two days' notice, Verdun alderman John Lennon stepped in and filled the role. The parade went west along Dorchester, up Fort and east past the reviewing stand which "took on a new and enhanced significance" that year. It had been moved to the front of the Ritz-Carlton Hotel at the suggestion of the hotel's functions manager, James Connelly, an enthusiastic member of the United Irish Societies. The heads of the various parish societies that formerly walked in the parade with their contingents now assembled on the reviewing stand as the parade passed by. In addition, the Grand Marshal now marched at the head of the parade instead of at the tail end.

1951 was also the 150th anniversary of the Act of Union, in which the Irish lost their Parliament. The first Irish ambassador to Canada, Sean Anthony Murphy, was the guest of honour at the dinner at the Queen's Hotel.

With the death of King George VI in February 1952, there were concerns that the parade might have to be cancelled because it fell during what was then the official period of mourning for the monarch. However, the new queen, who had visited Montreal as Crown Princess Elizabeth the previous year, declared that all events of a charitable nature, which included the parade, should go ahead as scheduled. That year organizers created a new position, that of Chief Reviewing Officer, to recognize the contributions to the

The reviewing stand at the Ritz-Carlton Hotel.

Irish community of someone who wasn't necessarily Catholic or of Irish heritage. The President of the Irish Protestant
Benevolent Society, J.J. Russell, was offered the position,
but was unable to accept, so a past president of the society,
William Bryant, took the salute in his place.

A patrol of the Temple of Karnak fought wind and
snow as the parade made its way down Sherbrooke Street.
An Italian contingent, the Comitato di Santa Giacomo, was
represented for the first time. Frank Hanley, who was the
acting mayor, upstaged the dignitaries, as he and Parade
Marshal Councillor J.A. Murphy waved to the crowds.

In 1953, Paul Emile Leger, who had been named a Car-
dinal of the Roman Catholic Church by Pope Pius XII in
January, celebrated the Green Mass at St. Patrick's Basilica

O'Donnell's King's Transfer Lines was the parade's
first commercial sponsor.

before the parade began on the afternoon of March 16. An
estimated 5,000 took part including the parade marshal,
William Minogue, the assistant director of the Montreal
Police Department. Joseph Cullen, Grand Knight of Montreal Council 284 of the Knights of Columbus, was Chief Reviewing Officer. At the St. Patrick's dinner, Mayor Houde was
given a collection of 100 volumes of Irish literature, including
15 books written in Gaelic.

Television was in its infancy in 1954 when the CBC
assigned cameras to cover the parade. To accommodate the
news reporters, Loye issued a directive prohibiting "outland-
ish headgear, paper streamers, or anything that might give the
parade 'a ragged appearance.'" That included drinking and

smoking. But winds of near-blizzard proportions howled around the marchers who took part in the mile-long procession. A 100-piece marching band came in from Toronto for the occasion and caught the attention of one editorial writer. "The winds blew, there was rain, drizzle, sleet and snow. Yet, they marched. Sleet blocked the instruments in their hands. Now and again, trumpets gave forth an uncertain sound and the tuba players staggered under their vast coils of metal as they strove to stay upright against the gale. Yet they played. It was man against nature in the St. Patrick's Parade. The Irishmen won." St. Ann's parish celebrated its centennial that year and a contingent of the St. Ann's Young Men's Society walked behind a float that carried an image of the church. George Bolton, President of the Holy Name Society, was the Grand Marshal and John Brennan, a patron of St. Ann's Church, was chief reviewing officer. The auxiliary bishop of Montreal, Lawrence Whelan was on the reviewing stand.

St. Patrick's Day in 1955 is remembered as a riotous event in every sense of the word. A street rampage occurred that evening four days after Montreal Canadiens superstar Maurice "Rocket" Richard had been suspended by Clarence Campbell from the NHL playoffs. Richard had been tossed out of a game against Boston but the Boston player who started the fight on the ice received a minor penalty. When Campbell arrived at the Forum for the game on March 17, angry fans set off Molotov cocktails, then trashed and looted storefronts along a 15-blocks radius around the Forum and caused hundreds of thousands of dollars' worth of damage. At least 50 people were arrested and 37, including 12 police officers were injured. Curiously, the flower shop in the Forum that had a large window display of shamrocks was spared. "Those shamrocks kept the rocks and bricks away from my window," declared the shop owner. The Irish Export Promotional Board declared an Irish Trade week across Canada that year and floats promoting Irish imports, sweaters, crystal, carpets and whisky were featured as a "hands across the sea salute to Ireland." Montreal's new mayor, Jean Drapeau, elected five months earlier on a campaign to clean up the city, accepted the invitation to be part of the promotion. Skies darkened on March 20 as the parade stepped off at three in the afternoon. A crowd of 35,000 bystanders braved a freak 10-minute snow storm to cheer the 6,000 people who walked in the parade led by a contingent of 250 uniformed city policemen. "They blew their bugles until their eyes bulged, and the cymbals rang in the air long after they passed," the *Gazette* observed. Judge Redmond Roche, who had commanded the Regiment de Maisonneuve during the war, and who was the National Union member of the Quebec legislature for Chambly, was chief reviewing officer. The oldest item in the parade was an 80-year-old jaunting cart.

At the celebrations in 1956, John Loye was recognized for his 25 years as President of the United Irish Societies. The city's deputy mayor, Mme. Eustache Letellier de Saint-Just, representing Mayor Jean Drapeau, was the first woman to walk the parade in an official capacity. Irish Ambassador Lee McCauley took the salute on the reviewing stand.

The first Queen's Pageant was held that year. It wasn't meant to be a beauty contest, but rather a three-round public speaking competition in which contestants of Irish descent had to articulate a broad knowledge of various subjects. Patricia Ann Craig was selected as the first queen to reign over the festivities. Col. John Redmond Roche, who had been chief reviewing officer in 1955 was grand marshal, and William P. Kierans, the chief reviewing officer.

The parade in 1957 was one of "green hats, green ties, green socks and a heavy foliage of green shamrocks." Twenty marching bands, including bands from Ottawa and Quebec City, boomed out traditional Irish airs as Angus McLean Gilday, the President of the Irish Protestant Benevolent Society, was dusted with light snow as he walked along the route. The Chief Reviewing Officer, William Hickey and Montreal's chief of detectives, Chief William Fitzpatrick took the salute as the float carrying the parade queen, Agnes O'Neill, glided past the reviewing stand.

The pipes and drums of the Black Watch (RCH), joined the parade in 1958 as 15,000 people lined the parade to see Marshal Frank Burns and Chief Reviewing Officer William Hickey walk down Sherbrooke St. Erin Shannon was parade queen.

"Impressive, dignified and decorous," was the way Irish Ambassador to Canada, Thomas Kiernan, described the parade in 1959. Kiernan was the Chief Reviewing Officer and watched as the two-mile parade took an hour to pass the reviewing stand in front of the Ritz-Carlton Hotel. The Grand Marshal was Dr. P. Nelligan, and Maureen Whooley, wearing velvet green robes over her fur coat, was the parade queen.

Chapter Fifteen

THE 1960S USHERED IN THE SO-called "*revolution tranquille*," a heady, not-so-quiet revolution in Quebec that began with the election of the Liberals in 1960 which sparked Quebec nationalism, led to cultural and political unrest, and ended with terrorist bombings and the kidnapping of a British diplomat and the murder of a Quebec cabinet minister.

The rhythm of the parade, too, changed over the decade as it increasingly became less of a parish march past and much more inclusive, commercial, secular and high-spirited. By the end of the 1950s, the French interests which owned the Ritz-Carlton Hotel added a 10-storey lateral wing to the building and no longer wanted to have the reviewing stand in front of the hotel's main doors. So, in 1960, the parade route moved from Sherbrooke St. to St. Catherine. Merchants along the main drag were invited to decorate their premises and "use this opportunity to add colour to the parade." Pedestrian crosswalks along St. Catherine were painted green; green martinis and green beer made their appearance in many of the downtown hotel cocktail lounges.

Governor General Georges Vanier and his wife were the honoured guests at the St. Patrick's dinner on March 17, 1960. Three days later, John Cronin, the Irish-born creative advertising director, with J. Walter Thompson and the president of the St. Ann's Young Men's Society, which observed its 70th anniversary that year, was grand marshal. The parade boasted 40 units and 16 marching bands that made their way through the rain, snow and sleet. Ed Coleman was the chief reviewing officer and Doris Kennedy, the parade queen.

The following year, former Prime Minister Louis St. Laurent and his wife were the honoured guests at the St. Patrick's dinner served at the Windsor Hotel. Mayor Jean Drapeau's right hand, Gerry Snyder, then a dynamic city councillor who would later bring major league baseball to the city, was grand marshal in 1961 and William Fay, Ireland's ambassador to Canada, chief reviewing officer. The parade queen was Betty McGrory.

St. Catherine Street was again at its "emerald best" for the 1962 parade, "here a Shanahan, there a shillelagh, and everywhere a shamrock." The 75-piece Army, Navy, and Air Force band, the largest brass band in Canada, was one of 18 bands in the parade. Kenneth McKenna was grand marshal and Rev. Jim O'Toole, pastor at St. Aloysius parish was chief reviewing officer. Patricia Browne was parade queen. Irish Diplomat William Fay, who had been reviewing officer the previous year, however, had reservations about the "element of clowning and buffoonery that many Irish people would find offensive, the green top hats, the shillelaghs, the green carnations, green whisky and even green traffic lanes—not to mention the festooning of everyone with a shamrock." What Fay had found especially undignified were the garish decorations on the tables at the St. Patrick's dinner, as well as the offensive nature of the sentiments expressed on St. Patrick's greeting cards.

After winning five consecutive Stanley Cups, the Montreal Canadiens were celebrated in the 1963 parade. Frank Selke, the club's general manager was chief reviewing officer, and Maurice "Rocket Richard" donned a top hat and walked through the rain in that year's parade. Dr. J. Kenney Mooney, the Habs' doctor, was grand marshal. Two siblings, Anna and Nuala Gavigan, competed in the competition for parade queen that year; Anna was selected as queen and Nuala served as one of the princesses in her court.

News of the wedding of Elizabeth Taylor and Richard Burton at the Ritz on Sunday, March 15, 1964, upstaged the annual St. Patrick's Parade which fought high winds as it made its way through the streets. The parade began to reflect the growing unbridled spirit of the "swinging" '60s. As journalist Bill Bantey noted, "Shamrock-laden top hats were swept away. Flags crackled in protest. [...] Band girls with bare legs marked time with greater gusto than usual. Bright sunshine brought a metallic glitter to the 25 bands and the floats." The parade was designed to promote ecumenical unity. Kenneth Maguire, the 8th Anglican bishop of Montreal, who had been a priest in Armagh, was the reviewing officer. Richard F. Walsh, President of the Federation of Catholic Charities was grand marshal. Bishop Lawrence Whelan was again on the reviewing stand, and Margaret McGregor was parade queen.

By 1965, the first stirrings of a separatist movement aimed at making Quebec unilingually French became apparent. And Frank Hanley, who somehow always

Frank Hanley

managed to keep his foot in both camps at the same time made headlines in the French media with his peppery speech in the Quebec legislature in which he declared that "The Irish would fight on the side of French Canadians to achieve justice within Canada."

Prime Minister Lester Pearson and Quebec Premier Jean Lesage were guests at the ball on the Friday before the parade. Lord Killanin, then the International Olympic Committee's chef de protocol and chairman of the IOC's press commission, was the guest of the St. Patrick's Society in 1965. He regaled 2,000 guests with his lighthearted speech which included self-deprecating remarks such as "The Irish are a fair people who never speak well of one another except on St. Patrick's Day." T. P. "Tim" Slattery, a prominent lawyer and historian who spent a lifetime studying the murder of Darcy McGee, was the parade marshal. Slattery was writ-ing his book about the trial of McGee's accused assassin James Whelan, *They've Got to Find Me Guilty Yet.* Eric Kierans, Quebec's revenue minister who had been dubbed "the socialist millionaire," was chief reviewing officer and walked ahead of the 27 bands and 45 floats including the one that carried Parade Queen Arleen Morrell.

The religious nature of the parade had been dwindling for a number of years, but 1966 marks the year the parade came into its own as a secular rite of spring. A proposal from the Ville Marie Wax Museum to promote a new exhibit in the parade commemorating the assassination of D'Arcy McGee threw plans for the 1966 parade into disarray. The museum was located along the parade route in McGee's old house at

1198 St. Catherine Street West, and had commissioned an effigy of the martyred McGee from Tussauds in London. In early February, museum director Blake Lilly suggested that the theme of the parade be "McGee Comes Home," and that his wax figure be driven down St. Catherine Street in a "vintage touring car."

It proved to be a public relations disaster.

The Irish Ambassador to Canada, John Bolton, thought the whole thing was in poor taste, coming as it did three years after the murder of the United States President, John F. Kennedy. "McGee may have been a great Canadian, a Father of Confederation, but his assassination has nothing to do with Ireland or with St. Patrick," Bolton wrote to the organizers. If McGee's effigy was to be in the parade, Bolton said point blank that he wouldn't attend. That year's grand marshal, Bryce Mackasey, the Liberal Member of Parliament for Verdun, agreed. If Bolton wouldn't attend, Mackasey wouldn't either. To add to organizing committee's headaches the Orange Lodge wanted to be included that year but was refused permission to do so. The idea of McGee's effigy was scrapped and "with harmony restored the parade went off without a hitch—not even a donnybrook." Mackasey marshaled the parade and Frank Hanley, who claimed to have been in every parade since 1916, rode a prancing palamino to mark his 50th anniversary as a celebrant. Veronica O'Shaughnessy, who was born in Scotland to Irish parents, presided over the festivities as parade queen.

In March of 1967, Montreal sparkled with anticipation as it prepared to play host to International and Universal

Exposition, Expo 67, and celebrate the centennial of Canadian Confederation. The president of the United Irish Societies, R.C. Cooper, hoped to invite U.S. Senator Robert Kennedy to ride in the parade, and if he couldn't accept, wanted his younger brother, Senator Edward Kennedy as "a stand in." The UIS also tossed around the idea of having Prime Minister Lester Pearson, whose parents were Irish immigrants, as grand marshal. But in spite of attempts to recruit a celebrity to do the honours, in the end, Rev. Patrick J. Ambrose, a social worker who had run Catholic Welfare Bureau for two decades, was named Marshal of the 1967 parade. Ambrose believed that caring for the poor and the marginal was as much of a calling as the priesthood itself. The loudest cheers that year, however, were reserved for the chief reviewing officer, Mayor Jean Drapeau, the man responsible for putting Montreal on the map. John Turner represented Prime Minister Pearson on the reviewing stand. Later all the dignitaries attended the ball at the Chateau Champlain where the 11th Marquess of Sligo, Jeremy Browne and his wife, the Countess of Altamont were among the honoured guests.

The 1968 parade is on record as one of the last innocent fun-fuelled demonstrations before the tumultuous decade of student unrest and political uncertainty that was to follow. Bishop Norman Gallagher, a former wing commander in the Royal Canadian Air Force and a former armed forces chaplain during the Second World War, the pastor of St. Patrick's was the chief reviewing officer. Judge R. J. Tormey was parade marshal, which may be why a unit representing lawyers and notarial professionals were among those who walked in the parade. The RCMP led the march followed by the Black Watch and Maureen McCabe was the reigning queen.

There was a small donnybrook as students held a protest demonstration on Phillips Square, but nothing like the violence that erupted in June when stones and Molotov cocktails were thrown at Prime Minister Pierre Elliot Trudeau during the Saint-Jean Baptiste parade.

In January 1969, students at Sir George Williams University staged a riot, and the choice of Rev. Patrick Malone, the innovative rector of Loyola College, as the grand marshal of the parade in March, was timely. Malone had transformed the jesuit college into one of the most progressive Catholic campuses in North America. He opened the college to women and appointed its first female chaplain. Malone believed that Catholic values could compete when tested against other beliefs. And he was negotiating the merger of Sir George Williams and Loyola into what is today Concordia University. Gerald O'Donnell, president of Kings Transfer Van Lines was the chief reviewing officer and Vickie McDonough parade queen. A contingent of the Royal Canadian Mounted Police headed the parade, and on the streets, crowds swilled green beer to help ward off the chilly wind. As the *Star* recorded, "It was more apparent than ever among the deep ranks of the spectators that Montreal is truly cosmopolitan. There are people of almost every conceivable nationality, many in native costume." As boulevardier Nick Auf der Maur put it, "Even the hippies went Irish. The long-haired and the bearded stood beside youngsters and oldsters to watch the pageant."

The political unrest continued. In June, the Saint-Jean- Baptiste parade was again disrupted when an effigy of Saint- Jean-Baptiste was decapitated. Twenty people were arrested. Then, in December the Santa Claus Parade was cancelled because FLQ terrorists threatened the Eaton's department store and refused to permit the 1970 Saint-Jean-Baptiste Parade to go down Sherbrooke St. and restricted Fête nationale celebrations to Old Montreal. For the next few years, it was uncertain whether the St. Patrick's Parade would be allowed to continue down St. Catherine Street. "The Fête St. Jean had been co-opted by the separatists. It no longer welcomed everyone and had become political and a threat to public security," reasoned Richard McConomy. "St. Patrick's Parade was inclusive, it welcomed everyone, including the separatists. But I think what really saved us from being shut down was that the Irish ran the only parade in town in which there was no likelihood of trouble."

Chapter Sixteen

DAVID DEEGAN, WHO WAS in charge of the 1970 parade, appealed to the various parish priests to use whatever authority they might still have to combat the rising tide of Quebec nationalism by sending delegations of all nationalities to the parade to show the strength of English-speaking Montreal. "Our French-Canadian friends make every effort to uphold their language, culture and religion," he wrote. "We of Montreal's Irish and English-speaking parishes seem to remain silent and invisible and let our acquired rights and traditions disappear through our own apathy and activity."

There were complaints that the green line wasn't painted down St. Catherine Street for the parade on Sunday, March 15, 1970. It was there but painted in such a dull deep green colour that no one could see it. Michael J. McCormick, who had come to Montreal from Calgary to work as the assistant to Seagram president Charles Bronfman, was the grand marshal. Albert David was chief reviewing officer. Brenda Reid was the parade queen.

In October 1970, terrorists kidnapped the British Trade Commissioner James Cross and murdered crusading journalist and Quebec's Labour Minister Pierre LaPorte. Shock gave way to an uneasy feeling about holding a parade the following year. The War Measures act was declared, and by March 14, 1971, all of those involved had been captured and brought to trial. The day before the parade, Paul Rose was convicted of LaPorte's murder. Strutting along in top hats, Parade Marshal John Carey, the Canadian manager of Ireland's Export Board who lived in Toronto, and Sam Maislin, head of Maislin Transport, the first Jew to walk as Chief Reviewing Officer, took part in Sunday's orderly parade. Parade Queen Deborah McHenry and her court rode on a new and elaborate flat, but the loudest cheers were reserved for the youngsters from the Leo's Boys Club in Pointe St. Charles.

In the evening after the parade, a drunken brawl involving about 50 people broke out at the Queen's Hotel. Although organizers claimed the parade was apolitical, the troubles in Ireland could not be ignored.

More than 200 men and women in the parade on March 19, 1972, wore black arm bands in mourning for the 13 unarmed civilians who had been murdered six weeks earlier by British soldiers in the Bogside, Derry. Many who took part were also saddened to learn of the death closer to home of the *Montreal Star's* Irish-born reporter, Denis O'Brien, who was killed in a car accident the day before on his way back from Toronto to cover the parade. Typically, it was the usual St. Patrick's Parade with prancing majorettes and top- hatted old timers. Justice Marshal Clarence Quinlan was grand marshal, and Bishop Leonard Crowley, the chief reviewing officer. Susan Murray was parade queen.

Roman Catholics observe the feast of Canada's patron

A freak storm couldn't stop the 1974 parade.
Photo by Garth Pritchard

saint, Joseph, two days after St. Patrick's Day. But on St. Patrick's Day in 1973, news broke that the heart of the now sainted Brother André who built the St. Joseph's Oratory in Montreal had been stolen from its reliquary in the shrine.

A life-sized statue of St. Patrick was roped to a car and driven through the streets on parade day, March 18. There were 20 marching bands and 12 floats but the parade queen, Deborah Tierney, almost didn't make it. She was trapped in an elevator in the Windsor Hotel shortly before the parade was to begin. It took firefighters 45 minutes to get her out. The acclaimed novelist and screenwriter Brian Moore recalled that if you overlooked the *à vendre* signs along the way, "St. Patrick himself could easily have mistaken St. Catherine

Street for the Emerald Isle as Montreal in his honour filled the air with shamrocks and shillelaghs and Irish tunes."

Retiring hotelier James Connolly was honoured as grand marshal. After leaving the Ritz-Carlton as functions manager, Connolly went to Malbaie to run the Manoir Richelieu where, according to one account, he "brought all his charm, enthusiasm and love of life to the Irish." Architect Joseph Dunn was the chief reviewing officer. Among the guests on the reviewing stand were Lord O'Neill of the Main and Lady O'Neill, whose family descended from the princes of Tyrone and remotely from Niall, the great 4th-century king of Ireland. Irish wolfhounds, "big enough to be wearing saddles," were popular with the crowd, the first time since 1851 that dogs were officially allowed to be in the parade.

The 150th anniversary parade, on Sunday March 17, 1974, pushed its way through a freak snowstorm "for the glory of God and the honour of Ireland." The wind was so strong that three floats were whipped to shreds and had to be removed from lineup before the parade ended. "It was like an arctic expedition," remembered Warren Allmand, the chief reviewing officer who was then Canada's Solicitor-General. John Quinn, a former New York State Senator and a senior executive officer of the Windsor Hotel, was the grand marshal. Parade Queen Maureen Ann McNally and her court were chilled to the bone by the time they took shelter on the reviewing stand.

By contrast, the parade the following year on March 16, 1975, was held on one of the warmest days ever. There were 50 floats, and thousands turned out to watch as Parade

Marshal Frank Phillips and the chief reviewing officer, the Liberal Member of Parliament for LaSalle, John Campbell, led the parade. Maureen O'Shea, a 17-year-old step dancer and student at Father MacDonald Comprehensive High School was parade queen.

An Irish contingent from Boston disrupted the 1976 parade on March 14, with such unruly behaviour, they were told not to return. "They were too drunk for a parade that has religion as its basis," explained parade official Brendan Deegan. The two-hour parade itself went off without incident, with a former mayor of Verdun and former Liberal member of the Quebec Legislature, George O'Reilly as grand marshal. Police officer Dan Yacovitch was chief reviewing officer, and Patricia Canty, the queen.

The election in November, 1976, of René Lévesque's Parti Québécois committed to Quebec independence galvanized the country, but ultimately would prove to be beneficial to parade organizers. The PQ's Minister of Culture, Louis O'Neill, recognized the historic attachment of the Irish to Quebec and went out of his way to reassure, (not always convincingly), the English-speaking Irish community that it had nothing to fear from the *souverainiste* option because three out of every 10 Quebecers were Irish. Just before the 1977 parade on March 20, O'Neill contributed $3,000 to the parade. Entrepreneur Ronald Toohey was grand marshal, and Richard Walsh, from the Federation of Catholic Charities, who had been marshal in 1964, was back, this time as chief reviewing officer. Kelly Rostek was parade queen. But Frank Hanley, who never seemed to miss a parade, rode in at the last minute on a pony to resounding cheers.

The first flag raising ceremony in Place Ville Marie on March 3, 1978, preceded the parade which took a longer route than usual on March 19. Parade organizer Norman Browne said the event demonstrated that the parade had become a symbol not only of Canadian unity but also of international unity. "It was a delight to watch the crowds; the intermittent snow flurries could have been confetti," Chris Bain wrote in the *Montreal Star*. The parade was marshalled by Patrick Fitzgerald Verdun. Mayor Lucien Caron was chief reviewing officer and 17-year-old Tracey Sweeny parade queen.

The Montreal Alouettes had won the Grey Cup football trophy in the Olympic Stadium and Miss Grey Cup, Saskatchewan's Laura Wedland, rode in the parade as well.

The Canadian Broadcasting Corporation provided live coverage of the parade on Sunday, March 18, 1979. Katie Malloch and Bob McDevitt provided colour commentary. The tumultuous decade came to an end as a record 185 units from Canada and the United States took part. Parade Marshal Martin Conroy and Chief Reviewing Officer John McConomy were joined in the walk by federal and provincial politicians, including the PQ's minister of electoral reform, Robert Burns; Liberal MNA, George Springate; labour lawyer, Brian Mulroney, who had just lost his first bid for the leadership of the Progressive-Conservative party to Joe Clark; and Bryce MackaseyThey were all cheered on by a crowd of 300,000 spectators.

Fashion maven Iona Monahan staged a ceilidh for Parade Queen Sandra Lynn Hume and her court.

"There was more of everything this year," remarked one bystander. "The St. Patrick's Parade is a lot like Christmas. Sure, you've seen it all and heard it all before, but you feel you lost something if you didn't have it."

Chapter Seventeen

ONE MONTH BEFORE THE 1980 St. Patrick's Parade, the city's blue-collar workers went on strike. Because of the labour strike, snow piled up on the streets and the green line down St. Catherine Street. wasn't painted in time for the parade on March 16. Armed with a compressor and 15 gallons of paint, media personality and sports columnist Ted Blackman and his friends stepped in to do the job themselves. Beer and blarney flowed as Brian Mulroney, who had lost the leadership of the Conservative party to Joe Clark in 1976, appeared in the parade marshalling votes for a convention in June that had been called to replace Joe Clark whose minority government had just been defeated in a non-confidence vote. The parade that year was an elaborate affair, with 168 entries, including 40 brass bands and 18 floats. Neil Willard, a gregarious Roman Catholic priest, who would soon be appointed a bishop, was chief reviewing officer, and Andrea Egerton, the parade queen.

Premier René Lévesque called a provincial election just before parade day in 1981 and the Liberals had high hopes that their leader, Claude Ryan, would easily defeat the separatists. Many felt Lévesque's government was doomed

The green line down St. Catherine Street wasn't painted in time for the parade, so sports columnist Ted Blackman and his friends stepped in to do the job themselves.

because it had lost the first sovereignty referendum the year before. Pierre Trudeau wondered aloud why anyone "would have the good sense to call an election against a man named 'Ryan' a week before St. Patrick's Day." Gerald Raymond, the mayor of LaSalle, was grand marshal, Peter McGlynn chief reviewing officer and Linda McEriaian parade queen. To everyone's surprise, in April the PQ was returned to power.

Prime Minister Trudeau walked in the 1982 parade on March 14 with a cup of Irish stew in his hand. An estimated 300,000 watched as Marshal Peter Bedard and Chief Reviewing Officer L. Cdr. Rev. Thomas McEntee, pastor of St. Edmund of Canterbury, led the parade, and Catherine Crow

161

was the queen. The absence of women from the United Irish Societies had been of concern to president Andrew Fogarty. In 1983, he invited Beverly Taugher (Rozek/O'Donnell), to become a member.

"To me the St. Patrick's Parade was like the Santa Claus parade," Rozek recalled. "We weren't supposed to have a drink to celebrate but everyone passed around a flask anyway." Rozek's paternal grandfather had been a professional Lacrosse player with the Shamrocks; she was a successful businesswoman working full time and wanted to know what becoming a member involved. "Andrew asked me if I would mind taking notes at the meetings and be the recording secretary. So, I joined and stayed on for many, many years," she said.

The 1983 parade was a two-hour affair marshalled by Irish historian Jake McConomy. It featured 31 floats and 40 marching bands. Brian Mulroney, then the Conservative opposition leader, sang Irish songs at the Hunter's Horn, but the biggest cheers were for nurses at St. Mary's Hospital who found themselves under attack from mean-spirited militants who had unfairly claimed the nurses had neglected to treat a terminally ill French-speaking patient in her own language. Michael Spears, a city police officer and a valuable member of the Erin Sports Association, was the chief reviewing officer and Suzanne Shannon was parade queen.

To mark the 150th anniversary of the United Irish Societies in 1984, women at last were allowed to attend the St. Patrick's luncheon. The parade broadcast live on CBC television that year was one of the smoothest ever, unmarred by public drunkenness, street brawls, or political controversy. It was ever expanding in its diversity with representation from various ethnic communities and was shedding its ingrained Roman Catholic connections. The Parti Québécois' minister of culture, Gerard Godin, a poet who had been jailed in 1970 under the War Measures Act, was on the reviewing stand with Chief Reviewing Officer Joe Sullivan as floats and marching bands made their way along St. Catherine Street.

The parade marshalled by Robert Larkin attracted 200,000 in -3°C temperatures and was described by reporter David Johnston as a windswept sea of green. "Clientele included elderly men with bumpy red noses, West Indians with green cardboard top hats that read 'Kiss me I'm Irish,' and flushed young women with hoarse voices and shamrocks on their faces, and excited children," all presided over by Parade Queen Linda McKeown.

By 1985, Brian Mulroney had become prime minister, and the reporting of his Shamrock Summit with United States President Ronald Reagan in Quebec City on March 17, 1985, upstaged the St. Patrick's Day Parade in Montreal, but the parade in Montreal went on with Bishop Leonard Crowley as grand marshal, Carolyn Byrne as parade queen, and Hugh McGlynn as chief reviewing officer.

City workers went on strike again in 1986, but in a gesture of public relations to win public opinion to their side, this time they painted the green line down St. Catherine Street. Gerald O'Donnell was grand marshal; Eric Molson, the chief reviewing officer; and Rosaleen Carroll, the parade queen

Prime Minister Pierre Trudeau enjoys a hot cup of Irish stew.

A sense of jubilation infused the parade in 1987. As Nick Auf der Maur, whose daughter Melissa was born on St. Patrick's Day in 1972, put it:

> [A] simple parade that over the past few years has become a genuine, spontaneous people's festival, one organized in a seemingly lackadaisical manner without the slickness, commercialism and professional promotion or the government subsidies that other 'popular' fetes seem to require. The Irish spirit is as deeply ingrained in Montreal's history as is the shamrock on its flag.

Gerald O'Donnell, who had been the chief reviewing officer in 1969, was honoured again, this time as parade marshal. Andrew Fogarty, a formidable presence in the Irish Catholic community was chief reviewing officer. Fogarty managed the Canadian War Assets Corporation in Newfoundland after World War II. When he moved to Montreal, Fogarty held a number of executive positions with the St. Patrick's Foundation, St. Patrick's Society and St. Patrick's Square.

Janice Campbell was parade queen.

The news that two British soldiers were beaten to death in Belfast by an angry mob attending a funeral for a member of the Irish Republican Army broke two days before the parade in 1988. The event known as the "corporals killings" sparked a small protest demonstration and demands that the public boycott the parade.

"We sympathize with the problems, but we don't get involved," said Tom Fitzgerald. "Our parade is a celebration, not a demonstration." There was never any question of cancelling the parade which went ahead with 37 floats and 35 marching bands and former United Irish Societies President Francis J Quinn, founder and president of the LaSalle Irish Society as parade marshal. Kirkland Mayor Sam Elkas, also the Liberal member of the Quebec National Assembly, was the chief reviewing officer, and Kimberly Amiot was parade queen.

There were concerns that a demonstration by the Mouvement Québec français, in favour of the French Language Charter, Bill 101, might disrupt the parade on March 12, 1989. But both events took place without incident. In fact, the St. Patrick's Parade attracted twice as many people as the nationalist demonstration, and when the Québec français march ended, a number of its participants showed up to cheer on the St. Patrick's Parade. Rev. Bill McCarthy, an Anglican priest and Korean War veteran, "who swore like a trooper and prayed like a saint," was honoured as parade marshal. McCarthy had run the Old Brewery Mission for more than three decades and being named marshal had, he said, been one of his life-long dreams. He described the honour as "happiness personified." Verdun's Mayor Raymond Savard was chief reviewing officer and Margaret Aherne, parade queen.

Gazette columnist Janice Kennedy complimented those who lined the sidewalks in "a state of array—or disarray"—-and applauded the parade itself for "the noise, general hokeyness and the occasional descent into Broadway Blarney."

But the trend was regarded with a jaundiced eye by some. Sports columnist Tim Burke, for one, lamented, "Where once St. Patrick's Day and the parade afforded a festive show of identity and strength for a group that could hold its own with the Protestants or the French, it has now become a harmless sham of quaint ethnicity."

Chapter Eighteen

BY THE 1990S, MONTREAL WAS able to boast that its St. Patrick's Parade had become the third largest on the continent; Only New York and Boston had bigger celebrations. But as the crowds along St. Catherine Street grew bigger and bigger, they became rowdier and rowdier. The pointed headline in the *Gazette* on Sunday, March 19, 1990, suggested that the atmosphere on the street had become "greener and meaner." Reporter David Johnston wrote about the sexist and vulgar hoots that greeted attractive women on the floats and noted that one float that encouraged revellers to say "no to drugs and alcohol" was roundly booed.

Liam Daly, the vice president of TMI Canada who produced the *Montreal Irish Show* on television was the parade marshal. Daly was the kind of guy who put green food colouring into his mashed potatoes on St. Patrick's Day. He was, he said, not a stereotypical Irishman. "The Irishman is always the guy with the big smile and the big heart who is always thrown out of the bar but is loved by everyone. Me, I'm the kind of Irishman who bursts into tears at sad tales and sad movies about Ireland." Valerie Shannahan was the parade queen.

These ladies, with their liquid refreshments, were charmed
by this police officer.

The St. Patrick's Day Parade on Sunday, March 17,
1991, attracted at least a half a million people, crowds ten
deep, "faces pale as cod's belly turned to the warm sun,"
as Jack Todd described it. It was a noisy affair, filled with
liquid refreshment, cheers, sirens and the crack of musketry
from visiting soldiers dressed in American Revolutionary
War uniforms. Jim Coleman, a veteran Montreal Urban
Community police officer who was awarded the Governor
General's medal for exemplary service, and former president
of the United Irish Societies, was the parade marshal.

For a number of years, the sashes used by dignitaries in
the parade had been made by a company in Toronto. In 1991,

someone in Montreal who did a lot of sewing was approached to do the job. But when the official sashes were presented at the Queen's Selection banquet, Elizabeth Quinn didn't think they were good enough to be worn. "They were dinky. Truly embarrassing," she said. "I couldn't see anyone walking around in them." Quinn approached the executive and volunteered to "fix them." Her husband, Fred Mackay, was a printer and provided her with the fonts needed to cut the felt lettering. Initially it took her about eight hours to make each one but the results in gold and green were so impressive that Quinn is now known as the "Sash seamstress." She takes great pride in making them not just for Montreal's parade, but over the years has been commissioned to turn them out for the executives in the St. Patrick's parades in Toronto and Quebec City. Her sashes made their first appearance in the 1992 parade when Montreal celebrated its 350th anniversary.

The parade was held on a frigid Sunday, March 15, so cold that as the *Gazette* pointed out, you could be forgiven for thinking Erin Go Brr. Yet more than 250,000 lined the streets in the -10C weather to watch. Fifty Veterans of the Foreign Wars came from Middleton, New Jersey, to take part in the parade. Mabel Denis (Fitzgerald) was the first female to be selected as a parade dignitary when she was named chief reviewing officer. Mabel was the den mother to the UIS and for many years worked under the radar as a volunteer before she became treasurer then vice president of the organization. Richard McConomy, a former Quebec batonnier and a genial lawyer with an impish wit, who had been legal advisor to the United Irish Society for a number

Mabel Fitzgerald was the first woman Chief Reviewing Officer.

of years was parade marshal. At St. Patrick's Basilica, which had been refurbished, Msgr. Russell Breen told those who attended the Mass that the occasion marked "a time when faith and culture are so intermingled, it is hard to pry them apart. It's a time of celebration for those of us with Irish blood and if you don't have any—God help you—pray for it."

A winter storm the evening before Sunday, March 14, 1993, threatened to halt the parade, but Tom Fitzgerald refused to cancel it. "It's going to go on. They'd hang me if it didn't." And go on it did. To Fitzgerald's surprise, even though it was -21C, "One hell of a crowd showed up."

Derek Deegan, an executive with Canadian Pacific and an award-winning athlete and coach, was grand marshal. Kelly Pierson was the queen. The theme of the parade was "Sharing Our History, "and it was more multicultural than ever with participation from the Italian, Greek, Spanish, Black and Mohawk communities. Boston cancelled its parade that year after Catholic authorities refused to let gay activists take part. But in Montreal, no such controversy has erupted. Parade organizer Tom Fitzgerald welcomed all comers, including LGBTQ groups as being free to register for the parade with the understanding that it was "a celebration, not a gay pride demonstration." (In fact, one year a strip club was given permission to enter a float). But it wasn't until 2011 that the rainbow pride flag made its debut in the parade when students from Concordia's Irish Studies Program marched with it without incident.

In 1993, a humanitarian award honouring Simon McDonaugh who organized the annual parade for almost 40 years as chief deputy marshal, was established. Maureen Kelly, a community volunteer who had prepared Christmas baskets for the United Irish Society for a number of years, was the first recipient. The Montreal Canadiens won the Stanley Cup in June. One sports commentator would point out that the only time Montrealers came together as one was for the St. Patrick's and the Stanley Cup Parades. But the 1993 Stanley Cup celebrations got out of hand and turned ugly. Montreal Urban Community Police Chief Jacques Duchesneau, who was on the reviewing for the 1994 parade, was relieved "to see so many people having a good time, a peaceful time, if you know what I mean," he said, alluding to the havoc that marred the Stanley Cup victory parade. Derek Deegan was grand marshal and Jennifer McKeogh parade queen.

The hit of the two-and-a-half-hour 1994 parade, which boasted 30 marching bands, was a large contraption that played bells and bagpipes and sent blasts of confetti into the air. It was designed in the shape of a harp by students at the McGill School of Architecture. Don Pidgeon, the historian of the United Irish Societies, was the grand marshal; Colleen Murphy, the parade queen; and Lt. Col. J.L. Andre DeQuoy, a World War II Royal Canadian Air Force veteran, the chief reviewing officer.

Montreal Mayor Pierre Bourque on foot and Police Chief Jacques Duchesneau on horseback, joined the hundreds of thousands who whooped it up for the parade on Sunday, March 19, 1995. LaSalle businessman Keith Mattics, the parade marshal and chief reviewing officer, and CJAD's sports director Ted Blackman, walked ahead of the

50 floats and 37 marching bands. The theme of that year's parade was "Peace in Ireland." Shelly Howe, a social sciences student at John Abbott College, reigned over the parade as queen.

"Living in Harmony" was the theme of the St. Patrick's Day Parade on March 17, 1996. Dancers from a local strip club had a float of their own as Grand Marshal Rev. Neil Willard, who had been a priest at St. Gabriel's for 21 years, and Police Chief Jacques Duchesneau as the chief reviewing officer, walked in the parade. Live donkeys and goats added to the cacophony of the 40 marching bands that led the way for Queen Jaime Kirnan.

Gazette columnist Peggy Curran was less than impressed with what had become a hedonist's holiday. "Back in the days when the parade was a parochial event, it was made up of mainly men in black top coats, high hats and white silk scarves following a banner naming their church," she wrote. "Now it is more cosmopolitan. Put a lid on hucksters selling green plastic bowler hats and shots of whisky. Ban drinking on floats … and here's a final revolutionary thought. Maybe just maybe, it is time to ask a woman to be grand marshal."

In 1997, a Polish dance troupe was featured in the parade. Leo Delaney, who had come to Canada from Dublin in 1953 was Grand Marshal in 1997. A graduate of St. Mary's College, Dublin, Delaney was active in the Irish community. He was a former chairman of the St. Patrick's Ball, published the *Canada Times,* and was involved with the Jeanie Johnson Educational Foundation. Terry Clahane, the choir director at St. Gabriel's Church was chief reviewing officer.

In 1994, Don Pidgeon, the historian of the United Irish
Societies, was the grand marshal.

The City of Montreal, aware of the parade's growing reputation as a tourist attraction, contributed $10,000 to organizers for the 1998 parade. The Mowhawks, Keepers of the Eastern Door, made their first appearance as they made their way through slush and swirling snow along 24 blocks of St. Catherine Street. on March 15, 1998. Mounted police rode horses. The grand marshal was Brian McKewan. Rev. Murray McCory, the pastor of St. Gabriel's church was to have been the chief reviewing officer, but he was called to Rome on business so Terry Clahane, who had been chief reviewing officer the previous year, represented McCrory.

The year 1999, marked the 175th anniversary of the parade. UIS Society President Margaret Healy was determined to give the proceedings "an extra push," by making it even more inclusive. She didn't think the City's $10,000 grant was sufficient and met with Mayor Pierre Bourque, who had just been re-elected to his second term and told him so. She didn't have to twist Bourque's arm very hard. Following her meeting with the mayor, the City of Montreal doubled its grant and chipped in $20,000 towards the cost of the anniversary parade. It didn't hurt that Bourque's special advisor to the anglophone community was Allan Patrick. An elevated wheelchair-accessible viewing area was installed, and organizers took advantage of new technology to live stream the parade on the internet. There was a shamrock shortage that year so the parade's grand marshal, BLG customs broker Jim Barriere, paid to have them imported from the United States. CBC television news anchor Dennis Trudeau, whose great-great-great grandparents were Irish, was the chief reviewing officer. The parade queen, Kate Fitzpatrick, also had deep Irish roots. Her great-great-grandfather captained the Montreal Shamrocks hockey team in the 1890s.

The parade that stepped off on Sunday, March 14, 1999, was the longest to date. "If the parade is like no other, it is because it has a little something for everyone," *Gazette* columnist Peggy Curran wrote:

> For traditionalists there are delegations from Montreal's Irish Catholic parishes and Irish clubs, ... so alongside the giant paper maché Celtic cross, you get Amnesty International, Green Mountain Boys, greyhound dogs, Klingons and Vikings. Wearing of the green isn't just a song, it is a mission statement. When it comes to parade regalia, there is no such thing as too much green.

The green blowout is always a celebration.

Chapter Nineteen

ALCOHOL HAD ALWAYS BEEN part and parcel of the festivities. There had often been floats that promoted Irish pubs and urged bystanders to support their local taverns. Green beer flowed. Barkeeps often boasted that they had a run on Guinness and Jameson's on parade day, and, one year, Mother Martin's ran out of whisky. But as one wag remarked, "By that time, no one could tell the difference anyway."

Carousing had grown exponentially as street crowds continued to swell. By 2000, it was common to see spectators openly knocking back alcohol as they stood in line on the sidewalks each parade day. *Gazette* columnist Jack Todd had written with dramatic foreshadowing that intoxicated crowds who lined the sidewalk, like the "obligatory idiot wearing a two-bottle batting helmet with a bottle of Blue on one side and a bottle of O'Keefe on the other. The helmet, we assume, was to keep him from splitting his skull when his head hit the pavement," were often more interesting than the parade itself. Under Steve Dowd's leadership, organizers took initial steps to deal with the problem of drunks along the route but with an estimated half a million people lining the sidewalks each year, public intoxication was becoming harder and harder to control.

In 2000, Robin Burns, a former NHL player from Montreal who spent most of his career with the Pittsburgh Penguins before starting a $100-million-a-year hockey equipment company, was grand marshal. Rob Braide, the general manager of radio station CJAD was the chief reviewing officer. But some of the loudest cheers that year were for Trent McLeary, whose career with the Montreal Canadiens ended earlier in January when he took a slap-shot to the throat. The parade queen was Nolan Arditi and on the reviewing stand Stephen Rea, the Irish actor perhaps best known for his role in The Crying Game, watched as Canada's Finance Minister Paul Martin, Quebec's Premier Jean Charest and Montreal Mayor Pierre Bourque passed by.

Finance Minister Paul Martin walks with Premier Jean Charest in the 2000 parade.

Busloads of Boston Bruins fans rolled into Montreal to attend a 2001 St. Patrick's Day game against the Habs. The Habs lost to the Bruins 3-2, but on the following morning, the Boston Irish in town helped boost the street crowd for the parade to more than 600,000. Beer was flogged openly in the streets as private investigator Terence Corcoran, the vice president ot the Canadian Security Agency, was honoured as Grand Marshal. John McDonaugh, who was named a member of the Quebec Basketball Hall of Fame that year, served as chief reviewing officer. Nadia Collette presided as parade queen over the unusually spirited weeklong festivities.

Mabel Ann Denis (Fitzgerald) was the first woman to be honoured as Chief Reviewing officer in 2002. Fitzgerald had worked behind the scenes for the UIS for years before she became treasurer and later a vice president. "It was long overdue. Who would have thought a woman other than the queen would ever be a parade dignitary?" she told the author weeks before she died in 2020. "They finally recognized the love and dedication of all of the ladies who were always working away in the background."

Wayne Hogan, who had been involved with the UIS for 35 years, was grand marshal. Parade Queen Kellyann Ryan, a 23-year-old political science student, echoed Fitzgerald's thoughts. "Being Irish is not just for one day. It means hard work and commitment every day of the year."

The celebrations that year were marred when an electrical engineering student at Concordia University slipped under the wheel of a parade float and had his legs crushed. Following the accident, new regulations requiring security to walk on either side of each float were put in place, and every float and flatbed had to pass inspection before it was allowed into the line-up. But the regulations could not control individual behaviour or prevent an even worse accident in the future.

The United Irish Societies sustained another blow later that year when Stephen Dowd, who had been in charge of putting the parade together for six years, took his own life in October just as preparations were underway for the 2003 parade. He was only 43. Dowd had been one of at least 20 members of the Quinn family to be involved with the parade since 1928. The society's first treasurer was Alderman Patrick Quinn, his daughter Helen was the first woman to be engaged as the society's secretary in 1945, his niece Elizabeth was the first recording secretary, one of his sons, Francis served as UIS president in 1965 as did his nephew, Joseph in 1996. (Later his niece, Elizabeth, and great nephew, Kenneth, would hold the same position.) In recognition of the family's long service to the UIS. a trophy to be awarded to the best military unit was donated in their name. The first recipient of the trophy was a no brainer: the pipes and drums of the Black Watch (RHR) of Canada. Dowd's cousin, Kenneth Quinn, who worked at Future Electronics, was recruited to replace him as organizing director and one of his first directives was to have the float carrying the queen moved closer to the front to accommodate television coverage.

A permanent Ukrainian contingent became part of the parade in 2003 when Dr. Michael Kenneally, the principal of the School of Canadian Irish Studies at Concordia University, and Ireland's consul general in Montreal, was grand marshal.

Larry Smith, who had been the Canadian Football League's commissioner before being named publisher of the *Gazette*, was chief reviewing officer. Erin Ashley McCarthy was parade queen.

In 2004, Tara Hecksher became the first Black woman to reign as parade queen. Hecksher's father was born in Dublin but lived most of his life in Nigeria. Tara came to Montreal to study economics and international development at McGill. She entered the competition because a friend with the United Irish Societies encouraged her to do so. As the float carrying her neared the end of the parade, a man doused her robes with white paint.

"It was absolutely horrible, the kind of horror when everything moves around you in slow motion," said one eyewitness. Hecksher was shaken but remained dignified. She dismissed the incident as an "accident." The racist attack was ignored by the mainstream media and the perpetrator was never caught. A giant inflatable shamrock two stories tall was the highlight of parade floats that year as Parade Marshal Bill Hurley who ran a popular pub on Crescent Street "to celebrate my Irishness," was cheered by the crowds. The chief reviewing officer, George Bosse, had been a Mayor of Verdun before he was elected to Montreal City Council, and was in charge of cultural heritage development, responsible for special projects in downtown Montreal.

It took 180 years, but in 2005, a woman was at last officially proclaimed grand marshal of the parade; Margaret Healy, a former President of the United Irish Societies, well deserved the honour. Her father, Thomas Patrick Healy, was the Liberal Member of Parliament until his death in 1957 and was Grand Marshal in 1943. Five decades later his daughter walked in his footsteps. She had a special "feminine" black top hat designed for the occasion. That year more than 20 Quinn family members walked together as a unit and continued to do so for the next five years.

In 2006, Brian O'Neill, a member of the Hockey Hall of Fame and executive vice president of National Hockey League for 25 years, was parade marshal. O'Neill, who died in 2023, had worked as an assistant to Clarence Campbell and spent much of his career trying to improve the standard of play in the National Hockey League where he was respected for being able to attain results without alienating people. The author of this book was chief reviewing officer. While there were perhaps more deserving candidates for the honour such as the *Gazette's* sports editor Patrick Hickey, pop culture critic Brendan Kelly, theatre critic Patricia Donnelly or columnist Colleen Curran, I didn't consider it as recognition for anything I had done, but as a reward to be shared with all of my newspaper colleagues. Walking at the head of a parade is an exhilarating experience that can go to your head until you realize that the applause and cheers are not for any one person but a collective round of cheers for the event itself. Also in the parade were Belinda Stronach, a Progressive-Conservative MP who had recently crossed the floor in the House of Commons to join the Liberals and who was rumoured to be in the running for the Liberal party leadership as well as two senators, Marcel Prud'homme and my cousin, Senator Rod Zimmer. I was grateful to the organizers for inviting my

In 2005, Margaret Healy was the grand marshal of the parade.

Scarlet-clad mounties always add a measure of colour
to the parade.

86-year-old mother to join me on the reviewing stand where
she was entertained by the Bloc Québécois leader Gilles
Duceppe, ever proud of his maternal Irish descent. Courtney
Elizabeth Mullins, an articulate environmentalist with a
commerce degree from McGill University, was parade queen
that year.

The green line normally painted down St. Catherine
Street. was erased by sand and salt following a 15 cm snowfall
the day before the 2007 parade. But there seemed to be no
end to the cheering as Quebec's Premier Jean Charest, PQ
Opposition leader Andre Boisclair and Gilles Duceppe walked
together in the spirit of the day. Bishop Anthony Mancini,
then the vicar general of the Archdiocese of Montreal, was
chief reviewing officer, and the last Roman Catholic bishop
to take part in the parade. Eight months later Mancini, would

be installed as the Archbishop of Halifax. Accountant Ted Harman, President of Accent Insurance Solutions, was grand marshal, and Andrea McGlynn, that year's parade queen.

There were fears that a highly publicised protest demonstration against police brutality in Montreal slated for March 16, 2008, would disrupt the St. Patrick's Parade. But both events unfolded without incident as bare-legged bagpipers in kilts marched in -13C weather and attracted 250,000 onlookers. Because it was Palm Sunday, another year of the so-called "purple shamrock," the Green Mass at St. Patrick's was cancelled because the liturgical calendar avoids such celebrations that day. (The same thing happened again in 2016, but St. Patrick's Day will not fall within Holy Week in anyone's lifetime until 2160.) Dr. John Meany, the mayor of Suburban Kirkland, was Grand Marshal, and Jim Barriere, who had been grand marshal in 1999, was back as a dignitary, this time as chief reviewing officer. Briana Yerbury, a member of McGill University's women's rugby team, was the reigning parade queen.

Canadians were gearing up for a federal election in 2008 when Justin Trudeau, who was then running as the Liberal candidate in the Montreal riding of Papineau, showed up at the parade. NDP leader Jack Layton and Bloc Québécois leader Gilles Duceppe were also among the line-up of federal poli-ticians. Layton, who would prove to be more popular than the Liberals in the election which followed in October, broke ranks and left the section reserved for politicos to become a one-man band. Not to be outdone, Trudeau (who had been booed when the parade began), quickly followed suit as CF-18 fighter jets roared overhead. Both began grandstanding before the crowds. Trudeau narrowly won his seat in the October election which saw the New Democrats make sub-stantial gains in Quebec.

The grand marshal of the 2009 parade David John O'Neill carried the cane that Inspector "Paddy" Lawton carried in 1933. Erin Mackasy was the parade queen that year.

Chapter Twenty

CROWDS HAD BECOME so boisterous and unruly that fears that a serious accident would happen during the parade had been mounting for several years. On the morning of March 13, 2010, a 20-year-old student at St. Pius X Culinary Institute jumped from the back of a float on a flatbed truck at the corner of St. Catherine and Metcalfe Streets. He was instantly crushed to death beneath its wheels. The coroner's report indicated the student's blood-alcohol content was four times above the legal limit. Dignitaries at the head of the parade, including Grand Marshal Jim Killin, Chief Reviewing Officer Jim Coleman (who had been Grand Marshal in 1991), and Parade Queen Katherine McKendy, were unaware that 40 units behind them were stopped in their tracks because of the accident. The assistant parade director, Patty McCann, witnessed the accident. "It was horrible. All of us who saw it ended up with post-traumatic stress."

Gazette reporter Patricia Donnelly, was nearby when it happened. "Time had stopped on that corner," she wrote. "The student's body had been completely covered (with a tarp). There were no efforts to resuscitate. Police, parade security, grim, uncertain. Yet just a block away the carousing continued, unabated. Binge-drinking young people stumbling in alleyways, carrying their drinks openly as if Montreal streets had become one sprawling bar."

Donnelly called for flatbed trucks to be prohibited from carrying floats in future parades. "It's time to update the St. Patrick's Parade for the 21st century, making it green in every sense of the word. With the exception of a limo or two for the aged or ailing, heavy motor vehicles can be dispensed with. Bicycles, horses and hybrid cars will do."

There were petitions to imitate New York's example and ban all motorized vehicles from the annual observance. That idea was not very practical. Instead, the United Irish Society devised an emergency plan to guard against future mishaps and teamed up with Éduc'alcool to produce a survival guide to the parade. "It is a fun guide that teaches responsible drinking and what the limits are," explained Kevin Murphy.

Any of the 2,000 or so participants caught drinking were automatically suspended from taking part in the parade for three years. Because of the fatality, the number of floats in the following year was reduced from 31 to 26 as 300,000 spectators who lined the sun-drenched route in 2011. Rev. John Walsh, the compassionate pastor of St. John Brebeuf parish in LaSalle, perhaps then better known as a CJAD talk show host, walked as grand marshal. Walsh was a true ecumenical leader, a priest for 45 years who promoted Christian-Jewish dialogue in Montreal. He also engaged in a number of charitable works and raised money to house the homeless. A man at ease with paupers, popes and prime

Andrew Fogarty was the oldest grand marshal in the history
of the parade

ministers alike, he was joined by a long-time friend, former Prime Minister Paul Martin.

"There is something about being Irish that defies explanation," said Walsh, who walked with his sister, Marlene. "I thought of all of the Irish who came before me, of grand-parents, and of my dad who always walked in the parade. I am sure our ancestors were proud of us as we walked the full length of St. Catherine Street." Brendan Deegan was the chief reviewing officer and Olivia Crawford parade queen.

Onlookers wearing shorts and sandals again lined St. Catherine Street in 2012 as temperatures on parade day reached a record high of 22C. Grand Marshal Paul Loftus, a freelance journalist and industrial psychologist, walked in the four-hour parade with his 13-year-old daughter, Mary Lynne. Loftus had come to Montreal from County Mayo and quickly integrated himself into the local community as president of the Montreal chapter of the Ireland-Canada Chamber of Commerce. He also co-founded the Irish Canadian Olympic Support Committee. His walk was dedicated to "those people who left Ireland during the Great Hunger but never got to enjoy this great country as I did."

The chief reviewing officer was Danny Doyle, and Keira Kilmartin, a 20-year-old medical student at McGill and a dancer, was parade queen.

In 2013, 92-year-old Andrew Fogarty became the oldest grand marshal in the history of the parade. Fogarty had been involved with the English-speaking Catholic community for seven decades and had walked as chief reviewing officer in 1987. A trustee of the St. Patrick's Foundation, he had been the past president who opened the St. Patrick's Society to women. Fogarty had served on the boards of almost every Irish community organization on the Island, including the St. Patrick's and Father Dowd foundations and was a former president of Catholic Community Services.

Don Pidgeon, the St. Patrick's Society's historian, was chief reviewing officer.

It was so bitterly cold for the 2014 parade that the bag-pipes with the Sons of Scotland Pipes and Drums froze in the -20C temperatures, the year that William O'Donnell, was grand marshal and Brian Mackenzie chief reviewing officer. The provincial Liberal leader, Phillipe Couillard, campaigning for the April 7 Quebec election, joined Mayor Denis Coderre on the reviewing stand. Sarah Murphy was the parade queen.

It was bitterly cold again next year but 250,000 braved the -25-degree temperatures on Sunday, March 22, 2015, for what was described as a "shamrockeriffic" parade.

Geoff Kelley, Quebec's minister of Indigenous Affairs, who had won his seventh election as the member of the Quebec National Assembly for the riding of Jacques Cartier when the Liberals were returned to office in Quebec in 2014, was parade marshal. Ken Quinn teamed up with Richard McConomy to provide colour commentary for the live television broadcast. They huddled under blankets and a pink comforter to ward off the chill. "It was damn cold, but memorable," recalled Quinn. "I prepared and prepared and McConomy spoke about stuff off the top of his head."

By then the parade was becoming a victim of its own

Richard McConomy and Ken Quinn were commentators for television coverage of the 2014 parade.

success. Grants from the City of Montreal and the provincial government covered about half the $100,000 budget needed to stage the spectacle, but the loss of a major sponsor combined with increasing expenses were of concern as the UIS started soliciting donations to underwrite its activities. The number of marching bands from outside the province was cut in order to economize.

"It is a very expensive endeavour to bring some of these bands in at our expense," explained Kevin Murphy. Still, there were 108 entries for the 2016 parade. Characters from the pop-culture movie *Star Wars* turned out to delight bystanders on Sunday, March 20. Paul Quinn, who owned the Irish Embassy tavern, was the parade marshal.

"All the lovely kids and families on the street and it's

just fabulous; it's great, great, great," Quinn observed. Lynn Doyle, co-founder of the Ciné Gael Irish film festival was chief reviewing officer and Samantha Cambridge, the parade queen.

A massive, mid-week snowstorm threatened to derail the parade on Sunday, March 19, 2017. But the streets were cleared and four new towering figures of St. Patrick, St. Andrew, St. George, and a Mohawk princess appeared for the first time in that year's observance as a salute to the city's 375th anniversary. Montreal Mayor Denis Coderre was honoured as parade marshal because of his unconditional support for the creation of a Black Rock memorial park and by virtue of his Irish ancestry. (Coderre's maternal ancestor, John McCabe, came to Canada from County Cavan in 1842.)

"We've had our share of fights, but the Irish community's presence means everything to the city, it is part of our DNA," said Coderre. Prime Minister Justin Trudeau walked again, this time with his daughter, Ella-Grace. "The parade is a reflection of the diversity that makes this country and this city so great," Trudeau declared. "Montreal is where it all comes together." Sister Dianna Lieffers, a nun with Our Lady of Sion who ran a food bank in Pointe St. Charles and was active in St. Gabriel's parish was chief reviewing officer. Lynne Loftus, who had been the 2012 parade with her dad when he was grand marshal, was queen.

Andrew Fogarty was back this time too, honoured as Irishman of the Year, and at 96, walked most of the way. An ice hockey team from Dublin was among the parade units and the Royal Canadian Mounted Police had the best marching unit.

The following year marked the 150th anniversary of D'Arcy McGee's assassination. Rev. John Walsh led an early morning commemorative service at McGee's crypt in Notre-Dame-des-Neiges Cemetery before the parade. St. Catherine Street had been ripped up for construction, so the 2018 parade had to be diverted along de Maisonneuve Boulevard. Grand Marshal Elizabeth Quinn, a former UIS President, compared that year's parade to the League of Nations.

"All ethnic groups are represented, everyone wears green, they all have their thumbs up and say they are Irish for a day. We have a good time. That's what it's all about." Ronnie James (who married the 2015 parade queen, Carly Meredith) was chief reviewing officer. Parade Queen Kathleen Brown-Vamdecruys, went on to join the Royal Canadian Mounted Police. The City of Montreal gave organizers $35,000 for the inconvenience of having to change the parade route because of the construction, and the following year, St. Catherine Street was again filled with spectators on Sunday, March 17, as a fly past of CF-18 jet fighters roared overhead and the 2019 parade began.

The first female mayor in the city's history, Valérie Plante (who had defeated Denis Coderre the previous October) walked in the parade with Grand Marshal Sean Finn, a taxation lawyer who had been the mayor of the South Shore community of Saint-Lambert, and a former chairman of the Metropolitan Montreal, Canadian and the Quebec Chambers of Commerce. Stand-up comedian Joey Elias was chief reviewing officer and Victoria Kelly the parade queen.

Ken Quinn was happy to see the parade back on St.

Catherine, even if the route was shorter. "You get used to doing the same thing the same way year after year," he said. "The set up on St. Catherine's is much easier. We like our traditions."

That tradition had to be put on hold because of the COVID-19 pandemic which claimed an estimated 14,000 lives in Quebec alone over the next two years, including those of a number of parade stalwarts like Andrew Fogarty, Margaret Healy, and Leo Delaney.

Although the 2020 and 2021 parades were cancelled, Montreal continued to honour the day. City Hall, the Olympic Stadium Tower, and Trudeau International Airport all were illuminated in green, or in the colours of the Irish flag.

Montreal joined Tourism Ireland's Global Greening initiative in 2020. A handful of diehards in Pointe St. Charles attempted to keep the parade going in 2021 with a "flash walk," along Wellington St. "Not lots of participants, but definitely lots of fun." said organizer Fergus Keyes, "and as in the past, a great reception from passing cars honking; and waving in support."

Chapter Twenty-one

A SMALL PARADE MADE a welcome return after a two-year pandemic absence on Sunday, March 20, 2022. With little time to prepare, it had been scaled down. There was no green line painted down Ste. Catherine Street, no floats, and only 500 participants marched instead of the usual 5,000. But the pipes and drums from the Montreal Black Watch were there. Dignitaries that had been selected for the 2020 parade remained in place. Chief Reviewing Officer Steve Garnett, head of the Montreal Auxiliary Fire Fighters, led the parade ahead of Grand Marshal Shawn O'Donnell, headmaster at Sacred Heart School, and Orla Mahon, who had been queen for two years, finally got to ride in the parade with her sister, Aveen, who was named princess in 2020. The absence of floats brought back memories of the parade's early days. "It used to be like this many, many years ago. There were church parades, and Irish groups and whatnot, when it wasn't as commercial," explained UIS president, Ken Quinn. "It's kind of like going back to our roots."

Mayor Valérie Plante, wearing an electric green raincoat, walked through the early morning drizzling rain with Liberal Cabinet Minister Marc Miller, the minister of Crown-

Indigenous Relations. It was a smaller parade than normal because there had been no normal for two years. Instead of shamrocks, many members of the United Irish Societies sported yellow and blue ribbons in support of Ukraine which had just come under attack by Russia.

2023 marked a full-scale return to the parade with marching bands, 80 floats that stretched for 2 km along Ste Catherine Street. The selection of that year's parade queen, Samara O'Gorman, made headlines because the roof of the convention hall collapsed during the event which chose the aspiring actress as queen. O'Gorman spent a year in County Galway on a scholarship to study Irish language and is fluent in the western dialect.

The day of the parade was also notable because it ended with the Chief Reviewing Officer Sterling Downey conducting the marriage ceremony of the Grand Marshal Tim Furlong to Timberly "Tim" Lampitt in front of the reviewing stand. Furlong had served as president of the Erin Sports Association for eleven years. Downey was a city councillor with a flowing white beard who founded the city's graffiti festival. He started growing the beard as a joke to match the bearded photographs of 19th century politicians. When he was named chief reviewing officer, he decided to cut it off as a fundraiser that collected $5,000 for the St. Patrick's Society.

Eight months after the wedding, Tim Furlong who had been living with cancer for several years, died.

Although 2024 is the 200th anniversary of the first parade, organizers have instead decided to celebrate the 200th

2023 Parade Queen Samara O'Gorman and her court

parade. "We've always gone by the numbers," explains UIS President Kevin Tracey. "The parade was cancelled for two years because of COVID-19, but basically, we weren't aware that parade was cancelled twice before that."

It will be up to a future executive to adjust the numbers and decide which year best represents the 200th parade either in 2028 or 2029 (depending on how they count the number of parades over two centuries) Tracey, who claims to be a distant relative of 19th-century Irish militant and newspaper publisher Daniel Tracey, says parade organizers are still recovering from the effects of COVID.

"The pandemic hit us pretty hard and there were other factors too. Our streets are a mess, there has been a financial impact, a lot of cost cutting, political strife among cultural groups." He believes, however that the parade has a future.

"The Irish in Quebec are a little different. It is our saving grace that we represent 40 per cent of Quebec's DNA. We are not a visible minority, the Irish roots run deep in French Canada. While it is true that Church no longer holds sway and has the power it once did, the parade will go on as long as the Irish are here."

A Mass of Anticipation for the 200th-anniversary parade will be held on Sunday, March 10, 2024 and the parade itself takes place on St. Patrick's Day, Sunday March 17. Mapping the route of the 2024 parade, however, proved to be a bit of challenge. St. Catherine Street was under construction and several routes were considered before the city and organizers agreed to have it go along de Maisonneuve Boulevard.

The chief reviewing officer will be Patty McCann, and

Mike Kennedy, a community leader who has served as a president of the United Irish Societies, vice-president of the Erin Sports Association, and vice president of Verdun Minor Soccer, is the designated grand marshal.

The author (left) rides in the 2015 parade with
Andrew Fogarty and Larry Smith.

ACKNOWLEDGEMENTS

I attended my first St. Patrick's Parade in 1969 and watched another 25 of them from the sidelines before I was invited to lead the one in 2006 as Chief Reviewing Officer. But my interest in the history of the St. Patrick's Parade was initially sparked by an article that I wrote for *The Gazette* 40 years ago about a Quebec civil servant, Yves Rafferty. Yves was a fifth-generation descendant of one John Rafferty who came to Montreal from Dublin in 1849, and who, a few years later, imported 200 tonnes of soil from Ireland and dumped some of it in his burial plot in Notre-Dame-des-Neiges Cemetery so that when he died, his bones could "co-mingle" with the soil of his native land. As he expressed it:

"Give me but six foot three, one inch to spare, of Irish ground

And dig it anywhere. And for my poor soul say an Irish prayer above the spot.

Give me an Irish grave mid Irish soil, with Irish grass above it anywhere.

And let some passing peasant breathe in prayer of the soul there."

What especially intrigued me about Yves Rafferty was that he had long been assimilated into Quebec's French culture. He worked in Longueuil, barely spoke English but identified as Irish. He was proof that the Irish diaspora has a mystical connection to its homeland, even if members have never been there. "When you are Irish, you are Irish no matter what language you speak," Rafferty told me.

The roots of the parade are more tangled than is often understood. It began as a showcase for Montreal's anglo-Irish, then a Catholic church event, and finally became one great green annual spring blowout. The 2002 parade was the biggest to date. $180,000 was spent that year putting it together. Instead of starting at Cabot Square, the parade route had to be shortened because the mustering point interfered with access to the Children's Hospital which at the time faced Cabot Square.

Early in March 2002, I was assigned by the *Gazette* to cover the parade and often dealt directly with Larry Smith who was then communications director for the United Irish Societies. That year, for the first time in parade history, a woman, Mabel Fitzgerald, had been chosen to lead the parade. Larry, of course was determined to get as much advance coverage but the city editor appeared to be ambivalent to Larry's pleas for a story. I wasn't especially surprised. In 1997, I had written a history of St. Patrick's Basilica to commemorate the 150th anniversary of the church. The book was published by Véhicule Press. The *Gazette* all but ignored the book and the anniversary until Lord Conrad Black who owned the paper, intervened.

There was little I could do on my own to sell a story to the editors of what has happening in the Irish-Catholic community. By 2002, the paper was beginning its slow decline. Readers, advertisers were disappearing and a new publisher had been hired to reverse the trend. The *Gazette* was now in the hands of a former football player who had been a running back with the Montreal Alouettes and went on to become a Commissioner of the Canadian Football League.

His name was also Larry Smith.

Everyone knew the name, but Smith had not yet arrived in the newsroom. As I was leaving the office on the Friday evening before the 2002 parade, the assignment editor received a curious phone call. I and three other reporters were suddenly assigned to give blanket coverage to the parade. "Larry Smith was on the line," he said. "He wants it covered." I didn't have the heart to tell him that it wasn't Larry Smith, the newspaper's new publisher that he had been talking to, but the other Larry Smith who was doing public relations for the United Irish Society.

Consequently, the paper, for a week in advance that year, was blanketed with reams of copy about the Irish. The Green Mass at St. Patrick's was featured and there was a full-page spread in the newspaper's community section. Columnists wrote about it. And the following year, the *Gazette*'s publisher, Larry Smith, was made chief reviewing officer.

Soon after that, I began doing serious research into the history of the parade. Records for the first five decades of St. Patrick's Day in Montreal were burned in a fire in 1872 but Andrew Collard encouraged the initial research by sharing his files with me when I wrote the history of St. Patrick's Basilica. Much of the initial detail was gathered by scrolling through 200 years of microfilm, reading the *Gazette*, the *Star*, the *Herald* and *La Presse*. Each parish contingent had its own marshal during the parades in the late 19th and early 20th centuries which gave rise to some confusion as to which of them was in fact the Grand Marshal. Newspaper accounts differ, so in some cases an educated guess was made.

This book was supported, in part, by a generous research grant from the United Irish Society. It could not have been written without the indispensable assistance of Ken Quinn, historian of the United Irish Societies and 2024 Irishman of the Year, who has been at my side almost every step of the way.

It would be impossible to list all of those who have contributed over the years to the book, but Don Pidgeon, Margaret Healy, Richard McConomy, Leo Delany, Andrew Fogarty, Lynn Doyle, Larry Smith, Rev. Barry Egan Jones and John Walsh all shared their insights and stories with me. Julie Jacques and Willow Little edited the manuscript and Peter Stockland helped me wade through Irish history. Mary McGovern and Moira Leblanc opened the archives at St. Patrick's Basilica, and Samara O'Gorman taught me how to turn an appropriate phrase or two in Gallic.

Mike Cronin's exhaustive history, The Wearing of the Green, proved to be an invaluable starting point; Kevin James' unpublished thesis, The Saint Patrick's Society of Montreal: Ethno Religious Realignment in a 19th Century National Society, Sean Connolly's On Every Tide: The Making and Remaking of the Irish World, were enlightening; and Christopher Klein's When the Irish Invaded Canada, was useful in piecing together how the Fenians infiltrated the parade ranks in the 1860s; Mark McGowan's The Wearing of the Green: Catholics and the Irish Identity in Toronto added to the perspective. Bert Archer at *The Gazette*, Ellen Gressling and Christopher Carr at Concordia University, and Mylène Bélanger at Exporail provided some of the photographic material.

A special thanks to Georgia Remond and Beverely Rozek for making St. Patrick Square my home away from home. As always, I'm grateful to my publishers Simon Dardick and Nancy Marrelli for their encouragement and for a friendship that has spanned two decades and seen eight of my books go into print. And to Stephane Lajoie-Plante who has kept me grounded, sort of, for three decades.

Blame me for any errors or omissions, which can be corrected in a future edition of the book.

May the gods continue to smile on the Irish and the parade organizers.

As they say in Gaelic, Go maire muid dhá chéad bliain eile.

APPENDIX

PARADE DIRECTORS
John Loye (1929-1942)
William Hickey (1943-1957)
Herb Tansey (1958)
Fred Taylor (1959)
William Hickey (1960-1964)
Ed Kelly (1965-1968)8
D'Arcy Boyle (1969-1970)
David Deegan (1971-1974)
Leo Pidgeon (1975-1977)
Norman Browne (1978-1979)
Tom Fitzgerald (1980-1996)
Stephen M. Dowd (1997-2003)
Kenneth W. Quinn (2003-2007)
Michael McCambridge (2008)
Beverly Murphy (2009-2011)
Patricia McCann (2012-2022
Kevin Dineen (2023 -)

GRAND MARSHALS
Ald. Thomas E. Fagan (1929)
Mr. P. O'Donnell (1930)
Toby Kavanagh (1931)
Patrick Doolan (1932)
Patrick Lawton (1933)
Christopher Carson, (1934)
Leo J. McKenna (1935)
T. Kilfeather (1936)
Dave Rochon (1937)
Mr. John J. Powell (1938)

Dr. L.P. Nelligan (1939)
Alderman R.F. Quinn (1940)
Hon. Francis Lawrence Connors (1941)
P.T. Lynch (1942)
T.P. Healy, M.P. (1943)
T.J. Guerin (1944)
Frank Hanley (1945)
Patrick Quinn (1946)
Rev. M.T.J. O'Brien P.P. 1948)
E.J. McManamy (1949)
Eddie O'Flaherty (1950)
J. Lennon, Grand Marshal (1951)
J.A. Murphy, Q.C. (1952)
Eddie O'Flaherty (1950)
Ald. J. Lennon (1951)
J.A. Murphy, Q.C. (1952)
William T. Minogue (1953)
F. Bolton (1954)
John A. O'Meara, Q.C. (1955)
Col. John Redmond Roche, Q.C. (1956)
Angus McLean Gilday (1957)
George O'Reilly Sr. (1958)
Dr. Lawrence Patrick Nelligan MD (1959)
Jack Cronin (1960)
Gerry Snyder (1961)
Ken McKenna (1962)
Dr. J. Kenny Mooney (1963)
Richard F. Walsh (1964)
T.P. Slattery, Q.C. (1965)
Bryce Mackasey, M.P. (1966)
Patrick J. Ambrose (1967)
Judge R D. Tormey (1968)
Very Rev. Patrick J. Malone, S.J. (1969)
M.J. McCormick, Grand Marshal (1970)

Mr. John Carey, Grand Marshal (1971)
Hon. Justice Clarence G. Quinlan, Q.C. (1972
James Connolly (1973)
John Quinn (1974)
Frank Phillips (1975)
George O'Reilly Jr. (1976)
Ronald Toohey (1977)
Patrick J. Fitzgerald (1978)
Martin Conroy (1979)
Brian Mulroney (1980)
Gerald Raymond (1981)
Peter Bedard (1982)
John McConomy (1983)
Robert T. Larkin (1984)
Bishop Leonard Crowley V.G. (1985)
Gerald O'Donnell (1986)
Wilfred Goddard (1987)
Francis J. Quinn (1988)
Rev. William McCarthy (1989)
Liam Daly (1990)
James P. Coleman, Grand Marshal (1991)
Richard McConomy, Grand Marshal (1992)
Derek Deegan, Grand Marshal (1993)
Donald Pidgeon, Grand Marshal (1994)
Keith Matticks, Grand Marshal (1995
Bishop Neil E. Willard V.G. (1996)
Brian McKeown (1998)
James Barriere (1999)
Robin Burns (2000)
Terence Corcoran (2001)
Mabel Ann Fitzgerald (2002)
Dr. Michael Kenneally (2003)
Bill Hurley (2004)
Margaret Healy (2005)

Brian O'Neill (2006)
Ted Harman (2007)
John Meaney (2008)
David John O'Neill (2009)
Jim Killin (2010)
Rev. John Walsh (2011)
Paul Loftus (2012)
Andrew W. Fogarty (2013)
William O'Donnell (2014)
Geoffrey Kelley, MNA (2015)
Mr. Paul Quinn (2016)
Denis Coderre PC (2017)
Elizabeth Quinn (2018)
Sean Finn (2019)
Shawn O'Donnell (2020)
Tim Furlong (2023)
Mike Kennedy (2024)

CHIEF REVIEWING OFFICERS
William Bryant (1952)
Joseph Cullen (1953)
John Brennan (1954)
Col. John Redmond Roche Oc. Obf (1955)
W.P. Kierens, Chief Reviewing Officer (1956)
William (Bill) Fitzpatrick (1957)
William C. Hickey (1958)
Dr. Thomas J. Kierens (1959)
Edmond Coleman (1960)
William P. Fay (1961)
Reverend James O'Toole P.p.(1962)
Frank J. Selke Sr. (1963)
Right Rev. Kenneth Maguire (1964)
Hon. Eric Kierans (1965)

John A. Belton (1966)
Mayor Jean Drapeau (1967)
Bishop Norman J. Gallagher (1968)
Gerald O'Donnell (1969)
Albert David (1970)
Mr. Sam Maislin (1971)
Most Rev. Leonard J. Crowley V.g. (1972)
Joseph Dunne M.r.a.i.c. (1973)
Warren Allmand M.P. 1974)
John Campbell M.P. (1975)
Dayacovitch 1976)
Richard F. Walsh (1977)
Lucien Caron MNA. (1978)
John Mcconomy (1979)
Rev. Monsignor Neil E. Willard P.h. (1980)
Rev. Peter Mcglynn P.p. (1981)
Rev.thomas D. Mcentee C.d. (1982)
Michael B. Spears (1983)
Mr. Joseph Sullivan Sr. (1984)
Hugh Mcglynn (1985)
Eric H. Molson (1986)
Andrew W. Fogarty (1987)
Mayor Sam L. Elkas (1988)
Mayor Raymond Savard (1989)
Sid Stevens (1990)
Jim D. Smith (1991)
Rev. Joseph Sullivan, Chief Reviewing Officer (1992)
Mr. Brian O'Neill Gallery (1993)
Colonel André Dequoy C.d. (1994)
Ted Blackman (1995)
Director Jacques Duchesneau (1996)
Terrance John Clahane 1997)
Rev. Murray McCrory (1998)
Dennis Trudeau (1999)

Rob Braide (2000)
John Mcdonaugh (2001)
Mabel Ann Fitzgerald (2002)
Larry W. Smith (2003)
Mr. Georges Bossé (2004)
Director Michel Sarrazin (2005)
Alan Hustak (2006)
Most Rev. Anthony Mancini V.g. (2007)
James Barriere, (2008)
Robert Larkin, (2009)
James P. Coleman (2010
Brendan Deegan (2011
Danny Doyle Sr. (2012)
Donald Pidgeon (2013)
Pipe Major Brian Mackenzie (2014)
Elizabeth Quinn (2015)
Lynn Lonergan Doyle (2016)
Sister Dianna Lieffers Nds (2017)
Ronald "Ronnie" James (2018)
Joey Elias (2019)
Steve Garnett (2020)
Councillor Sterling Downey (2023)
Patty McCann (2024)

PARADE QUEENS
Patricia Ann Craig, 1956
Agnes O'Neill, 1957
Erin Shannon, 1958
Maureen Whooley, 1959
Doris Kennedy, 1960
Betty McGrory, 1961
Patricia Browne, 1962

Anna Gavigan, 1963
Margaret McGregor, 1964
Arlene Morell, 1965
Veronica O'Shaughnessy, 1966
Clare Leonard, 1967
Maureen McCabe, 1968
Vickie McDonough, 1969
Brenda Reid, 1970
Deborah McHenry, 1971
Susan Murray, 1972
Deborah Tierney, 1973
Maureen Ann McNally, 1974
Maureen O'Shea, 1975
Patricia Canty, 1976
Kelly Rostek, 1977
Tracey Sweeney, 1978
Lynn Hume, 1979
Andrea Egerton, 1980
Linda McErlain, 1981
Catherine Crowe, 1982
Suzanne Shannon, 1983
Linda McKeown, 1984
Carolyn Byrne, 1985
Rosaleen Caroll, 1986
Janice Campbell, 1987
Kimberley Amiot, 1988
Margaret Aherne, 1989
Valerie Shannahan, 1990
Kimberley Anne Tyrell, 1991
Kelly Pierson, 1992
Jennifer McKeogh, 1993
Colleen Murphy, 1994
Shelly Howe, 1995
Jaime Andrea Kirnan, 1996

Amanda Elizabeth Hoover, 1997
Maureen Ring, 1998
Kathryn Fitzpatrick, 1999
Jennifer Nolan-Arditi, 2000
Nadia Collette, 2001
Kellyann Ryan, 2002
Erin Ashley McCarthy, 2003
Tara Hecksher, 2004
Stephanie Glezos, 2005
Courtney Elizabeth Mullins, 2006
Andrea McGlynn, 2007
Briana Yerbury, 2008
Erin Mackasey, 2009
Katherine McKendy, 2010
Olivia Crawford, 2011
Keira Kilmartin, 2012
Alyssa Caughy, 2013
Sarah Murphy, 2014
Carly Meredith, 2015
Samantha Cambridge, 2016
Mary Lynne Loftus, 2017
Kathleen Brown-Vandecruys, 2018
Victoria Kelly, 2019
Samara O'Gorman, 2023.

UIS PRESIDENT'S CHAIN OF OFFICE
John I. Mccaffrey (1929-1930)
Herbert Potter (1931-1932)
John Loye (1933-1957)
John Lucey(1958)
Martin Greene (1959-1960)
Patrick Quackenbush (1961-1962)
John J. Kenny (1963-1964)

Francis J. Quinn (1965-1966)
Richard C. Cooper (1967-1968)
Patrick J. Patrick J. Fitzgerald (1969-1970)
George O'reilly Jr. (1971-1972)
Robert T. Larkin (1973-1974)
James P. Coleman(1975-1976)
David Deegan (1976-1977)
Donald Pidgeon (1978-1979)
Wilfred Goddard (1980-1981)
Norman J. Browne(1982-1983
D'arcy C. Boyle (1984-1985)
Bernard Woffenden(1986-1987)
Bryan Scott (1988-1989)
Patrick O'connell (1990-1991)
Mabel Fitzgerald (1992-1993)
Michael Spears (1994-1995)
Joseph Quinn (1996-1997)
Margaret Healy (1998-1999)
Elizabeth Quinn (2000-2001)
Robert Mckay (2002-2003)
Sheila Showers (2004-2005)
Larry Smith (2006-2007)
Marlene Demers(2008-2009)
Kenneth W. Quinn(2010-2011)
Michael Kennedy(2012-2013)
Beverly Murphy (2014-2015)
Danny Doyle (2016-2017)
Paul Loftus (2018-2019)
Patricia Mulqueen (2020-2022)
Kevin Tracey (2023-)